THE WISDOM OF GOD

THE WISDOM
of GOD
AN OUTLINE OF SOPHIOLOGY

SERGIUS BULGAKOV

Preface by
FRANK GAVIN

Angelico Press

Cover design by
Michael Schrauzer

WITH SINCERE GRATITUDE

TO ALL THOSE

IN

AMERICA AND ENGLAND

WHO

HAVE MADE POSSIBLE

THE PUBLICATION OF THIS BOOK

NOTE

The author's grateful thanks are due to the Rev. Patrick Thompson, the Rev. O. Fielding Clarke and Miss Xenia Braikevitch for their kind services in translating this work.

CONTENTS

PREFACE

UNDER the impact of the several Oecumenical Movements our modern religious world has been undergoing rapid modifications. In view of the swift action of political truth, it is a fair question to ask ourselves whether ecclesiastical and theological developments have at all kept pace with the times. This is peculiarly the question circumstances address to present-day Christendom. This same question might be phrased in different ways : Are we growing in awareness and sensitiveness ? Do we see, feel and know the older tradition in its radical richness ? How near have we of to-day, who span continents with aeroplanes and centuries with the facile superficiality of what is in Reality little more than a " bird's eye view ", come really to terms with the insights and knowledge which the East has still to offer to the West ?

In several respects this book can be of enormous benefit to us of the Occidental rather than the Oriental Christian Tradition. In the first place it puts before us a God-centred rather than a man-centred universe. Ever since the Reformation

9

Western Christians have been much more concerned about themselves than about God even in reference to them. Perspectives have been grievously distorted. We stand in need of a restorative and of a spiritual repristination.

Again, the West has been decidedly sceptical about the place of reason in the scheme of God's things. Here is offered a wholesome corrective : God, who is the God of all, is the God of Plato and Aristotle as well as of St. Paul and St. John. A healthy rationalism is as important as a salutary mysticism in understanding his bounteous feelings toward mankind. The Old Testament is not to be depreciated in acknowledging the New, nor is the Old solely a Book of one race but the literary and spiritual record of the soul's travail in the whole of the world of men's thinking and feeling.

Finally, the scope of God's dealings with us means a progressive revelation. It is not—needless to say—God who progresses : it is ourselves—in perception, comprehension and awareness. So Fr. Sergius's essay has a peculiar relevance to those of us to-day who would ascribe final authority to the permanent and unchanging, but can only come to perceive it in the terms of our own thinking and powers of understanding. That this monograph may so serve is the ardent wish of

FRANK GAVIN.

INTRODUCTION

INTRODUCTION

ANYONE who has visited the church of St. Sophia in Constantinople and fallen under the spell of that which it reveals, will find himself permanently enriched by a new apprehension of the world in God, that is, of the Divine Sophia. This heavenly dome, which portrays heaven bending to earth to embrace it, gives expression in finite form to the infinite, to an all-embracing unity, to the stillness of eternity, in the form of a work of art which, though belonging to this world, is a miracle of harmony itself. The grace, lightness, simplicity, and wonderful symmetry of the structure account for the fact that the weight of the dome and even of the very walls seems to dissolve completely. An ocean of light pours in from above and dominates the whole space below —it enchants, convinces, as it seems to say : I am in the world and the world is in me. Here Plato is baptized into Christianity, for here, surely, we have that lofty realm of his to which souls ascend for the contemplation of ideas.

13

But as Plato's pagan Sophia gazes upon herself she learns to recognize herself in the Divine Sophia and, indeed, this church is an artistic proof of her existence and of her reality, spread like a protecting canopy over the world. It represents the last, silent revelation of the Greek genius, bequeathed to the ages, concerning Sophia, the Wisdom of God. Yet this marvel of architecture, though designed in a theological age in obedience to the will of the Emperor-theologian, remains without any obvious relationship to the theology of Justinian's epoch. It is a torch kindled for the benefit of subsequent ages. The dome of St. Sophia crowns and, as it were, summarizes all the theological creativity of the epoch of the Oecumenical Councils. What is the inner meaning of this church of St. Sophia, the Wisdom of God, which is like the swan song of the universal Church in the city of the New Rome? Is it merely a chiselled allegory, such as the churches dedicated to Peace, or Faith or Hope? The building of this church is a definite landmark in the creative activity of the epoch. For from that time churches dedicated to Sophia began to be built both in Byzantium and in Slavonic countries, with a wealth of mysterious and elusive symbolism. Undoubtedly they are churches dedicated to Christ, but to Christ in the aspect of Sophia—

to Christ-Sophia. What then does this imply? Byzantine theology as such has left behind no explanation of that to which this ecclesiastical architecture bears witness. It only bequeathed its hieroglyphic sophiology, as a theological problem, to the generations which succeeded it.

Nor was this theological problem taken into account or understood by old Rome, the *civitas Dei* as once the *civitas Romana*. There the universality of the Church was looked upon as a kind of spiritual citadel, the *imperium Romanum*, an organization of ecclesiastical authority culminating in the person of the Roman pontiff. The heavenly dome of St. Sophia, which had been suspended so far as it were in mid-air, here came to rest on an hierarchical foundation. The dome was no longer the symbol of eternity but of finite limitation. Everything was now defined, determined, coordinated and co-related under the supreme authority of Christ's representative on earth. Thus in the West the message of her pre-eminence enshrined in the churches of St. Sophia was narrowed. In the East, on the other hand, such obstacles never existed. When the faith of Christ was first blazed abroad by the missionaries of Byzantium, there came to the northern land of the Russian Tsardom (the " Third Rome "), together with Christianity, this mysterious and as yet undisclosed revelation of Sophia enshrined in the hieroglyphics of ecclesiastical architecture.

The first capital of Russia, Kiev, " the mother of Russian towns ", was the first to adorn itself in the eleventh century with a cathedral of St. Sophia. After this a growing number of churches was so dedicated as the Russian Church, and the influence of the state and of culture in general spread to the North. Moscow, the free city of Nijni-Novgorod, Yaroslavl and other towns, began to build their own churches dedicated to Sophia, the Wisdom of God. Here, too, as in the past, the theological implications of this symbol remained long hidden as a sacred mystery, though there is some partial disclosure of them at this time. It is true that this does not apply to theology, which in the backward conditions of the nation at this period was practically non-existent, but only to the further development of sacred symbolism. The sophianic symbol was first disclosed to some extent in the establishment of the day of the feast of title. These festivals are associated with a different range of ideas from those of Byzantium. The churches of St. Sophia in Russia, as a general rule, have their feasts of title on feasts of our Lady (in Kiev, the day of her Nativity ; in Novgorod and other places on the day of her Assumption). Secondly the texts of special services to Sophia, though not, it is true, very numerous, are highly significant. In this way we see that in the interpretation of Sophia, along with the Christological emphasis—which corresponds to the *Divine* Sophia —there emerges another, Mariological, emphasis, which corresponds to the *creaturely* Sophia, to the glorification of the creature. Even more significant are the sophiological symbols employed to depict Divine Sophia in the theology of colour and imagery. Here the most complicated and involved dogmatic compositions, only with difficulty capable of definite interpretation, embody the devout contemplation of the unknown makers. These icons have been accepted and authorized by the Church and are preserved to this day.[1] But these memorials of symbolic sophiology remain dumb, and though their meaning must have been clear at the time when they were composed, in our time, which lacks sophianic inspiration, they often remain enigmatic and partially incomprehensible relics of a former age. Scholastic theology commonly abandons the whole field of research into the lofty symbolism of sophianic churches and icons, together with the appropriate texts of divine worship, to the realm of archeology, as something essentially antiquated, or else

---

[1] *See* the photographs of icons of Sophia in Van der Mensbrugghe, *From Dyad to Triad*. London, 1935.

interprets it somewhat unsympathetically as a theological misunderstanding, the result of the unduly elaborate allegorizing of Byzantium, or its naïve imitation in Russia. All this wealth of symbolism has been preserved in the archives of ecclesiastical antiquities, but, covered by the dust of ages, it has been of no use to anyone. The time has come, however, for us to sweep away the dust of ages and to decipher the sacred script, to reinstate the tradition of the Church, in this instance all but broken, as a *living* tradition. It is *Holy Tradition which lays such tasks upon us.* It is a call neither to superstitious idolatry, nor to rationalistic contempt, but rather to creative understanding and development. Our own particular time with its special revelations and destiny has a peculiar call to this task.

The theme of Sophia never had any place in Western theology, either in the Middle Ages, or at the period of the Reformation, in spite of the intense theological ferment of the time. Though there is no doubt that Western theology constantly hovers on the brink of sophiological problems, yet the general context of the main problems of the Reformation and the Counter-reformation, with their exclusive emphasis on questions of personal salvation, of grace and of faith, was on the whole unfavourable to further dogmatic development, and particularly to a consideration of anthropology in its connection with cosmology, which is a special characteristic of sophiology. Protestantism shewed itself particularly barren in this sphere, for it narrowed tremendously the whole range of theological problems. This is particularly true of modern Protestantism, both of the " liberal " variety with its rationalistic adogmatism and historicism—*Leben-Jesu-Forschung*, and of the " orthodox " variety which reintroduces with new vigour all the limitations of its original world-outlook. Unfortunately the sophiological barrenness of Western theology influenced Eastern theology also in a negative direction, for, generally speaking, Eastern theology was subject to influence from this quarter. This resulted in a certain divergence between the true wisdom of the Church on the one hand and the rationalistic forms of theology on the other. To-day we are compelled to re-establish the connection.

Quite unexpectedly and apart altogether from any link with the Eastern tradition of the veneration of Sophia, we observe the beginning of teaching on the *Jungfrau Sophia* in the West in the seventeenth century, in the doctrine of Jacob Boehme, the mysterious cobbler of Berliz. Boehme is perhaps the greatest genius amongst German thinkers. Together with Eckhard, he represents the secret dynamic of the philosophy of Hegel and Schelling, of F. Baader and the romanticists. He had a tremendous influence on his contemporaries as well as on succeeding generations both in Germany and beyond it; for example, in England. In particular this applies to his peculiar doctrine of Sophia which is closely linked with his trinitarian theology. We may here add that an English mystic of the eighteenth century, Dr. Pordage, who wrote a series of remarkable treatises on Sophia, was thus influenced by Boehme's sophiology. This Western sophiology is primarily distinguished by the fact that already at this stage it came to realize the vital nature of the problems involved, and gave rise to a whole range of valuable and penetrating ideas on this subject. Nevertheless it cannot altogether be accepted by modern Orthodox sophiology, though this latter must give to it its due. The works of Boehme, Pordage and others were diligently studied by Russian Freemasons at the end of the eighteenth and the beginning of the nineteenth centuries. The translations of these works, in spite of the prohibition of the censor, were published and read in Russia and undoubtedly had a lasting influence on Russian thought. However, modern Russian teaching on Sophia does not derive from these sources, but from Holy Tradition, which silently pervades the whole history of the Eastern Church.

We should remember the fact that in the history of Russian religious thought the nineteenth century is characterized by its exceptional sensitiveness to such problems as the religious meaning of history, of creativity, of culture. This theme finds expression in the wording of the title of a work published by one of the earliest representatives of this line of thought, A. M. Bukharev (the Archimandrite Theodore) : *Orthodoxy in its Relation to Our Time.* The questions relating to the religious justification of culture and of creativity which were raised by the Reformation and by humanism and could only find a solution there in secularization, were in turn experienced, and in a far more painful way, by Russian thought. This process occurred, however, not so much within the sphere of official theology, which was insufficiently developed for such a task and was, in addition, fettered by official scholastic orthodoxy, as among the representatives of literature and art. Artistic creativity was deeply conscious of its religious sources. Gogol was literally consumed by his search, and by his attempt to make of the whole of his creative work a true sacrifice offered to God. The life of the Archimandrite Theodore was destined to become a continual tragedy as

a result of his prophetic seeking for new ways of
life and creativity.   This ascetic monk, one of the
greatest men of prayer, found himself in spiritual
conflict with the ecclesiastical environment in
which he lived.   He returned to the status of a
layman because he found that only at the price
of this immense sacrifice could he procure for
himself the right to follow freely his own particular
way of service.

The problems raised in the works of Gogol and
Bukharev are further illumined in a new way in
Dostoievsky, with his constant search for the way
to that Kingdom of God in the world, which he
foresaw as the future destiny of Orthodoxy.
Besides this we observe in Dostoievsky a profound
feeling for " mother earth ", for the cosmic aspect
of the Church, together with the anthropological
revelation found in the Church and a vivid
apocalyptic interpretation of history.   We should
also mention in this respect several of our greatest
poets who were gifted with special insight into
the mysticism of the natural world : especially
Tiutchev, the poet of cosmic chaos ; Fiet, who was
very much akin to him ; Baratinsky and others.
At a time when the majority of the Russian in-
telligentsia was carried away by a superficial
positivism or, at best, by Tolstoy's limited moralism, a real spiritual renaissance was taking place

in Russian Orthodox thought in this small exclusive circle. Yet another such solitary thinker
was Fedorov, who bore real marks of greatness in
spite of certain paradoxical and enigmatical elements in his make-up ; he interpreted Christianity
as the " common cause " of the resurrection of
the ancestors by their descendants, in the power
of Christ, and in the name of the Holy Trinity.
Although in a certain sense isolated, yet spiritually
(and even historically) he undoubtedly belongs
to this general trend of thought.

Towards the end of the nineteenth century this
quest at last begins to find expression in a theology
the very basic characteristic of which lies in its
teaching on Sophia, or sophiology. Vladimir
Soloviev (1853–1900), is the first representative
of this theology, the first Russian sophiologist.   In
his treatise *Dissertations on God-manhood* (1883)
which was printed in one of the leading Church
journals, he gives a philosophical and theological
formulation of the doctrine of the Wisdom of God.
He expounds his doctrine in numerous articles
and books, in particular in *La Russie et l'église
universelle*, 1885.   Nevertheless it should be pointed
out here that Soloviev's doctrine of Sophia is
undoubtedly syncretistic : side by side with ancient Orthodox tradition we can detect elements
derived   from   the   ancient   gnostic   systems,

together with the obvious influence of Western
sophiology in the writings of Boehme and others.
All this is further complicated by his own poetic
mysticism.   In his poetry Soloviev is indeed very
far from the Orthodox conception of Sophia.
This aspect of his world-outlook had a profound
(and far from valuable) influence on the subsequent generation of poets such as the gifted Blok,
Biely and certain others, who expound in their
poetry themes for the most part of an erotic-
gnostic character concerning the feminine principle.   It is also obvious that Vladimir Soloviev
had a tremendous influence on Dostoievsky ; this
is particularly noticeable in the latter's prophetic
utterances concerning " mother earth " and the
" free   theocracy " of the future.   Soloviev's
religious outlook had an inescapable influence on
the thought of subsequent generations, whether
those who submitted to it did so consciously or not.
Personally, though I do not share his gnostic
tendencies, I regard Soloviev as having been my
philosophical " guide to Christ " at the time of a
change in my own world-outlook, when I was
moving " From Marxism to Idealism "[1] and, indeed, even further, to the Church.

It is very important to emphasize this general

[1] Under this title a symposium of my articles was published in
1895–1903.   One of the most prominent places in it is occupied by an
article on Soloviev.

link between Soloviev and all the preceding currents of Russian thought, for his Christian philosophy in a certain sense embraces them all.[1]
There is a direct line which leads to Soloviev
starting from the Slavophil theology of Khomiakov
and continuing through the other thinkers I
have mentioned. All the living Russian religious
thinkers of our time have been influenced directly
or indirectly, positively or negatively, by sophiology, S. N. and E. N. Troubetzkoy, Berdyaev,
Zenkovsky, Karsavin, Florensky and others. Fr.
Paul Florensky, formerly a professor of the Moscow
Theological Academy, puts the problem of sophiology in an absolutely Orthodox setting. In his
well-known work *The Pillar and Ground of the
Truth* (The Church) he gives in the chapter on
Sophia an interesting theological interpretation
of the facts of iconography and liturgy referred
to above, and further illuminates it by his own
ecclesiology. This book produced a profound
impression in Russian theological thought and led
to much discussion. Its sophiological ideas became an inseparable part at any rate of the
problems raised by Russian religious thought.
I myself have developed my own position in a

---

[1] There is only one peculiarity in Soloviev's outlook which separates
him from this tradition, namely, his " Romanizing " recognition of
the primacy of the Pope, in which recognition he saw the ancient
tradition of the Church.

series of books, at first mainly philosophical, such
as *The Philosophy of Economics*, 1910, *The Light
that Never Fades*, 1917, *Die Tragœdie der Philosophie*,
and later in a series of theological works published abroad.

Russian religious thought finds itself in an
unfortunate position in the Christian world ; it is
still an undiscovered continent for Christendom
as a whole, which remains in a state of blissful
ignorance of our " barbarous " tongue (the
tongue, however, of some of the greatest writers
and of poets who are world-famous). It is only
by chance that certain things from the treasury
of Russian thought (by no means the most
valuable and authentic) rise to the surface of the
spiritual vortex of European life. These strike the
European by their peculiarity, so that he goes on
to ascribe the general spiritual atmosphere which
they share to the individual or the work in
question. In the same way the Bolsheviks when
confronted with an ignorant " Intourist " are apt
to take credit to themselves for such things as
the Russian winter, the Russian Volga, Russian
art, and so forth. From our standpoint, we
Russian Europeans, when watching the manifestations of European thought, are often struck
by the fact that trends of thought which appear
to us elementary, of small importance, and, to

be frank, entirely devoid of originality, acquire the significance of historical events and lead to the formation of " schools " producing in time a whole literature. (This, of course, does not apply to purely scientific research, where the predominance of the West is obvious.) But this attitude is particularly irritating to us at the present time in a period of otherwise developing inter-confessional intercourse.

A Russian proverb says " One cannot love to order " ; nevertheless it is at least the duty of Western Christians to *know* us as we are, if only for the reason that so far no other Church has had to experience the fiery trials through which we have passed, together with the spiritual revelations which they conceal. And if the general attitude of the West in relation to Russian thought may still be expressed by the rule, *graeca sunt, non leguntur,* we on our part are called to form a sort of " novitiate ", endeavouring to render at least the main currents of our thought accessible to the West in some concise form. The present outline of Sophiology pursues this course. It has been specially compiled for the Western reader with the secret hope of arousing his interest and urging him to become acquainted with the main works bearing on the subject.

The main purport of this essay is to expound the

doctrine of Sophia, the Wisdom of God. This doctrine is at the present time responsible for a sort of ideological ferment even in our own Orthodox *milieux*. It has already evoked a hurried condemnation on the part of some of the hierarchy, in spite of the fact that the whole problem is only on the threshold of dogmatic consideration. As a result of the atmosphere of sensation or scandal thus created around the doctrine of the Wisdom of God, the Western reader has already become acquainted with such words as " Sophia " and " Sophiology ". For him, of course, these words are tinged with the peculiar exotic Oriental flavour of " gnosis ", and, indeed, smack of every sort of rubbish and superstition. No one seems to suspect that in this controversy the underlying problem is one which has a profound bearing on the very "essence of Christianity," that it is a problem which is even now being discussed by the whole of Western Christendom. The real point at issue is that of the Christian vocation as it is related to the very nature of Christianity ; it is the problem of a dogmatic Μετανοία, nothing less than a change and a renewal of men's hearts. The doctrine of Divine Sophia has nothing to do with putting forward any new dogma, and certainly cannot be described as a new heresy within Christianity, although such is

the attitude adopted by certain " guardians " of
the faith, who see in complete stagnation the only
guarantee of a true faith and dread all new ideas
accordingly.

Sophiology represents a theological or, if you
prefer, a dogmatic, interpretation of the world
(*Weltanschauung*) within Christianity. It is characteristic only of one trend of thought within
Christianity, and that one which is by no means
dominant in the Orthodox Church, in the same
way as, for instance, Thomism or " Modernism "
exist within Catholicism, or liberal " Jesuanism "
or Barthianism within Protestantism. The sophiological point of view brings to bear upon *all*
Christian teaching and dogma, beginning with
the doctrine of the Holy Trinity and the Incarnation and ending with questions of practical
everyday Christianity in our own time, a special
interpretation. It is untrue to affirm that the
development of the doctrine of the Wisdom of
God leads to the denial or undermining of any
part of Christian dogma. Exactly the reverse is
true. Sophiology accepts all the dogmas acknowledged as genuine by the Orthodox Church
(though not those teachings which have been
accepted through scholastic misunderstanding,
and, frequently, forced on the Church from
outside). Wherein, then, does this sophiological

point of view consist, and in what way can it be applied to the fundamental teaching of Christianity? This essay is an attempt to give a short answer to this question. The introduction can only indicate quite shortly the general lie of the land.

The central point from which sophiology proceeds is that of the relation between *God* and *the world*, or, what is practically the same thing, between *God* and *man*. In other words we are faced with the question of the meaning and significance of God-manhood[1]—not only in so far as it concerns the God-man Himself, the incarnate Logos, but precisely in so far as it applies to the theandric union between God and the whole of the creaturely world, through man and in man. Within Christianity itself there is a never-ending struggle between the two extreme positions of dualism and monism, in a constant search for truth, which can only be found in the synthesis of God-manhood.

There are two opposite poles in the Christian attitude to life, which are both equally untrue in their onesidedness. These are, firstly, world-denying Manicheism, which separates God from

[1] This is the title which Vladimir Soloviev gave to his articles on sophiology—*Dissertations on God-manhood*. I have called my principal theological work in the same way *On God-manhood*—Part I. : *The Lamb of God* ; Part II. : *The Comforter* ; Part III. (in preparation) : *On Things to Come* (Ecclesiology and eschatology).

the world by an impassable gulf and thus makes
the existence of God-manhood out of the question;
and, secondly, an acceptance of the world as it
is, combined with submission to its values, which
is termed " secularization ". We notice the
former attitude in various, at times very un-
expected, combinations, mostly in cases where a
profound and serious religious attitude, a sense
of the reality of God, confronts man with an
" either, or "—*either* God, *or* the world. Thus in
choosing God man is constrained to turn away
from the world, to despise its works and values,
and to leave the world to itself and to its own
creativity in a state of alienation from God. We
come across such a-cosmism or even anti-cosmism
on the one hand in a trend of thought which has
historically prevailed in Orthodoxy—in the
" pseudo-monastic " outlook on the world, and
on the other hand in orthodox Protestantism
which likewise so insists on God's transcendence
to the world that the world is in effect deprived
of God.

The second attitude or tendency—the secularization of life—only indicates the general spiritual
paralysis of modern Christianity, which is, in
practice, powerless to direct or to control life.
Instead it submits to the existing order of things.
Such worship of the *status quo* shows that it has no

answer to the problems of life. Moreover, if
" salvation " is interpreted as a flight from the
world, and is at the same time associated with a
servile attitude towards it, we cannot be surprised
that the world turns away more and more from
such Christianity, and comes to regard itself and
its own life as constituting its own standard of
values. Such is modern atheism, which really
represents a deification of the world and of men,
and which is a special form of paganism. It is
not—as it frequently claims to be—the *zero* of
religion, but a *minus* of Christianity.

Christianity is at present powerless to overcome
this cleavage, this gulf between religion and the
world, which is apparent in modern life, for the
gulf exists not only outside, but within Christianity itself. Attempts to co-ordinate Christianity
with life (in so far as, in Roman Catholicism, this
is accomplished on the basis of subjecting the
world to a powerful organization of the Church)
are really nothing more than an attempt to
amalgamate two incongruous bodies, which can
not in fact be united, since each insists on its
own exclusiveness or totalitarianism. " Social "
Christianity finds itself in the same tragic pre-
dicament in so far as it also represents a sort of
adaptation, a peculiar form of opportunism,
without a *dogma* of its own. It strives to become a

sort of " applied " Christianity, a " Nicaea of ethics " to use the phrase of Archbishop Söber-blom. But the very conception of " applying " Christianity only confirms the absence of a genu-ine *dogmatic* Nicaea together with a certain readiness to compromise with life, a retreat from it or coming to terms with it, which is in no sense a creative leadership and inspiration of life. So far Christianity has followed in the train of life, lagging behind, without assuming any leadership. Furthermore, how can one lead in regard to something which one does not accept, in which one does not believe, towards which one's attitude is merely that of missionary adaptation, of philan-thropy or of moralism ?

Social Christianity, engrossed with its practical aims, has not as yet faced its dogmatic problem, namely, that of justifying the world in God, as a contrast to excommunicating it from God, which is what is preached and confessed in practice at the two opposite poles of Christianity, both in the Orthodox Church and in Protestantism. Is there a ladder between heaven and earth and do the angels of God ascend and descend upon it ? Or is this ladder only a convenient emergency exit for those who wish to be " saved " by forsak-ing the world ? Is our Lord's Ascension into heaven the very last, and, so to speak, culminating

act of our salvation ?   Or is there something else
that follows after it, something new, in the second
coming of Christ into the world, the Parousia,
which is not only judgment but at the same time
the beginning of a new, eternal abiding of our
Lord on earth ?

The answer to these questions has been given
long ago in the Christian faith, but it has remained a dead letter, it has not, so to speak, become a living reality.   This answer is contained in
the fundamental dogma of Christianity concerning
God-manhood.   The creaturely world is united
with the divine world in Divine Sophia.   Heaven
stoops towards earth ; the world is not only a
world in itself, it is also the world in God, and God
abides not only in heaven but also on earth with
man.   Our Lord says of himself : " All power is
given unto me in heaven and in earth " (Matthew
xxviii. 18).   God-manhood represents a dogmatic
call both to spiritual ascesis and to creativity ; to
salvation from the world and to a salvation of the
world.   This is the dogmatic banner which should
be henceforth unfurled with all power and glory
in the Church of Christ.

The dogma of God-manhood is precisely the
main theme of sophiology, which in fact represents nothing but its full dogmatic elucidation.
Why exactly this is associated with the doctrine

concerning the Wisdom of God and how this connection applies will become evident to the reader
in the course of the present work, which gives a
short summary of the doctrine of sophiology as it
is developed by the author, and will act as a guide
to his larger works.

Our modern age stands in need of a new apprehension of the dogmatic formulae preserved by
the Church in its living tradition. Moreover it
cannot be overemphasized that there is no single
dogmatic problem that does not at present need
such re-interpretation. And at the very heart of
things there stands, as of old, the basic Christian
dogma of the Incarnation, of the Word made flesh;
in the dogmatic setting bequeathed to us by
Chalcedon. The roots of this dogma penetrate
to the very heart of heaven and earth, into the
inmost depths of the Holy Trinity and into the
creaturely nature of man. " Incarnationism "
even now stands as the main fact of dogmatic self-
determination in Anglicanism, and in Protestantism also—let alone in the most ancient Churches
such as the Orthodox and the Roman Catholic.
Do people, however, sufficiently realize that this
dogma in itself is not primary, but derived ? In
itself it presupposes the existence of absolutely
necessary dogmatic assumptions in the doctrine of
God and man, of the primordial God-manhood.

These presuppositions are in fact unfolded in
sophiology. The same would apply to an even
greater extent to another dogma of God-manhood,
namely, that of Pentecost. This dogma, though
accepted, remains comparatively speaking but
feebly elucidated in dogmatic thought. It involves the descent and the abiding of the Holy
Spirit in the world in connection with the Incarnation. This connection as well as the power
of Pentecost in the one God-manhood is also
disclosed by sophiology.

To go even further, the fundamental and still
insurmountable difficulty so far in our age in
the striving of the Churches towards unity, is
the lack of dogma concerning the essence of the
Church as such. We are not concerned for the
moment with the external attributes of the
Church, its canonical or liturgical aspects, but
with what the Church *is* in herself. What do we
mean by the reunion of the Churches in one
Church ? Is this a " pact " or an act, that is a
manifestation of the one Church as a revelation of
God-manhood, as Sophia the Wisdom of God ?
Until the consciousness of the Church can reach
this depth of self-determination, all oecumenical
" pacts " will be in vain. Again and again will
the separated Churches dash in vain against the
walls which divide them, in a tragic realization of

their helplessness, in face of the objective impossibility of genuine reunion. There is, nevertheless, one true way, which is that of learning to know and understand the Church as revealed God-manhood, Sophia the Wisdom of God.

We will not refer here to the numerous theological questions of a more special nature, which acquire a new light in the doctrine of the Wisdom of God. We will confine ourselves to mentioning one more. Never before has the Christian conscience been so pressingly confronted with questions concerning man's destiny in history and beyond its limits, man's creativity and his responsibility to his own God-manhood. History unfolds itself before us as an apocalypse ; the apocalypse as eschatology ; the " end " as fulfilment ; Our Lord's second coming in the Parousia as His meeting with the Church : " And the spirit and the bride say, Come ! Even so, come Lord Jesus ! " (Rev. xxii. 17, 20).

Are the curse of secularization, as well as the anaemic Manichean denial of the world, symptoms of weakness, of the " failure " of historical Christianity, or are they but the darkness before the dawn, which awaits the rising sun of the coming day ? Is the world God-manhood in process of accomplishment, the Wisdom of God becoming manifest, the " woman clothed with the

sun " (Rev. xii. 1) even though still driven by the
dragon into the wilderness, or is the world itself
only a wilderness, " the empty house ", forsaken
by the Lord ?

Two forces struggle in the world in the guise of
two basic tendencies, that of cosmism and that of
anti-cosmism, the two disintegrated aspects of the
one divine-human theocosmism. Historically,
secularization was introduced into the world by
the Reformation and the Renaissance, which
represent two parallel turbulent streams of the
same main current—of what we may call, however
contradictory such a definition may sound—anti-
cosmic cosmism. The acceptance of the world by
Humanism was a reaction against its non-
acceptance, which only left it a right to natural
existence. We are confronted in this process by
a bad " dialectic " of unresolved contradictions,
which burdens and exhausts our time.

But such a " dialectic " in no sense represents
the last word of wisdom. We need a true
Christian ascesis in relation to the world, which
consists in a struggle with the world out of love for
the world. We must discover how we can overcome the secularizing forces of the Reformation
and of the Renaissance, not in a negative way or
" dialectically ", which is in any case merely
theoretical and powerless ; but in a positive way

—through love for the world. But again we repeat that this can be accomplished only through a
change in our conception of the world, and
through a sophianic perception of the world in the
Wisdom of God. This alone can give us strength
for new inspiration, for new creativity, for the
overcoming of the mechanization of life and of
man. The future of living Christianity rests with
the sophianic interpretation of the world and of its
destiny. All the dogmatic and practical problems of modern Christian dogmatics and ascetics
seem to form a kind of knot the unravelling of
which inevitably leads to sophiology. For this
reason, in the true sense of the word, sophiology is
a theology of *crisis*, not of disintegration, but of
salvation.

And finally, in contemplating culture which has
succumbed to secularization and paganism, which
has lost its inspiration and has no answer to give
to the tragedy of history, which seems in fact to
have lost all meaning—we realize that we can find
a spring of living water only by a renewal of our
faith in the sophianic, or theandric meaning of
the historical process. As the dome of St. Sophia
in Constantinople with prophetic symbolism portrays heaven bending to earth, so the Wisdom of
God itself is spread like a canopy over our sinful
though still hallowed world.

THE DIVINE SOPHIA IN THE HOLY TRINITY

THE DIVINE SOPHIA IN THE HOLY TRINITY[1]

THE dogma of the Holy Trinity consists in two basic postulates. The first affirms the triune character of the Deity, " trinity in unity " and " unity in trinity ". The Father, the Son, and the Holy Spirit, who are three distinct divine persons, together constitute one God. The second postulate is concerned with the consubstantiality of the Holy Trinity, which has but one substance or nature ($o\dot{v}\sigma\acute{\iota}a$ or $\phi\acute{v}\sigma\iota\varsigma$), *substantia* or *natura*. This dogma is most clearly expressed in a Latin Creed of the fifth century, the *Quincunque Vult*, the so-called Athanasian Creed, the authority of which is recognized

[1] *See* my previous studies on this subject (in Russian) : *The Light that never Fades.*—Chapters on the Trinity (from the Journal *Orthodox Thought*, I–II) ; *Hypostasis and Hypostatic Nature* (from the Symposium in honour of P. B. Struve). *On God-manhood :* Part I, *The Lamb of God*, Paris 1933, Ch. I, para. 2–3, pp. 117–130 ; Part II, *The Comforter*, 1936, para. 1–6, p. 6–63.

by the Eastern as well as by the Western Church.[1]

The first part of the dogma, that is, the doctrine of the relationship between the three hypostases with their hypostatic qualities and distinctive features, has been to a certain extent elucidated in the process of the Church's dogmatic creativity. But the other side, the doctrine of the consubstantiality of the Holy Trinity, as well as the actual conception of substance or nature, has been far less developed and, apparently, almost overlooked.

Moreover, we should note here that whereas we find the names of the three persons of the Holy Trinity in the Bible, the actual expressions " substance " or " consubstantiality " are not biblical. The term was brought forward and used at the Council of Nicaea as the result of great dogmatic activity, in the endeavour to find in his consubstantiality (ὁμοούσιος) with the Father a suitable expression for the idea of the divinity of the Logos. Later this term was extended to

---

[1] . . . *unum Deum in Trinitate, et Trinitatem in unitate veneremur. Neque confundentes personas, neque substantiam separantes.* Alia est enim persona Patris, alia Filii, alia Spiritus Sancti ; sed Patris et Filii et Spiritus Sancti una est divinitas, aequalis gloria, coaeterna maiestas.

The dogma of the consubstantiality of the Holy Trinity is expressed in different ways in the Orthodox liturgy. As an illustration we may notice the two following " ejaculations " of the priest :

    1. " Glory be to the Holy, Consubstantial, Life-giving, and Undivided Trinity now and for ever. . . ."

    2. " For Thine is the Kingdom, the power and the glory, of the Father, and of the Son, and of the Holy Spirit. . . ."

the whole Trinity, and the usage became well-established in the theology of the Cappadocian fathers and particularly of St. Basil the Great. Still later its use became general in the Eastern Church and it was largely employed by St. John of Damascus.

The term itself is adapted from the philosophy of Aristotle, who distinguishes between the " first " and the " second " substance in things ; between the *concrete* being, in which the essence, comprising certain " universals ", becomes specifically individuated ; and the *abstract* concept of essence, devoid of such specific character, and therefore lacking such real being of its own. Aristotle applies this scheme to all individual being, whether it be a stone or an angel, a thing or a man. The same method is applied by St. Basil the Great and St. John of Damascus to the elucidation of the doctrine of the Holy Trinity, the one divine essence being here individuated in three hypostatic relations, fatherhood, generation and procession.   Meanwhile in Western theology (with Augustinianism) the substance or essence in itself, yields precedence to the three hypostases, these being determined in their being through an interrelationship of origin (as opposed one to another).

We thus see that substance both in the East and in the West is interpreted purely as a philosophical abstraction, and utilized to achieve a logical solution of the trinitarian dogma. " Substance " provides doctrinal construction with a kind of ideological starting point. Such a conception cannot embrace the divine revelation with regard to the one common life of the Holy Trinity, of God in three persons. The dogma of consubstantiality which safeguards the unity of the Holy Trinity, thus remains a sealed book so far as we are concerned—for in a religious sense it has been neither assimilated nor unfolded.

The Bible, however, though it never alludes to the abstract conception of substance, does give us revealed teaching on the life of the triune God. In point of fact this teaching seems to have been little noticed and most certainly has not been utilized in trinitarian theology, in particular as regards the application to the doctrine of the substance of God of the biblical revelation of Wisdom or Sophia, and of the Glory of God. In this particular respect the liturgical consciousness of the Church is superior to the dogmatic, for the earliest liturgical texts have included such revelation in the text of hymns, lessons, and doxologies.[1] The *lex orandi* bore witness in itself to the *lex*

---

[1] Even the Athanasian Creed, as we have already seen, speaks of *una divinitas, aequalis gloria, coaeterna maiestas*. These expressions, however, have something of a rhetorical air, and are not usually interpreted as authoritative dogmatic formulae.

credendi. This witness, however, was disregarded by theology until the middle of the nineteenth century in Russia, when there were fresh stirrings of sophiological thought.

We find teaching about the Wisdom of God (hòkmah, ἡ Σοφία τοῦ θεοῦ) in the first instance in Proverbs. Chapters i.–x. obviously make use of this term to express wisdom as a quality—i. 7 ; ii. 6, 10 ; iii. 13, 14–18 ; iv. 5 ; vii. 4 ; ix. 10. There is a double meaning in i. 22–23 and iii. 19–20. But there is no longer any doubt that Ch. viii. 22–31 contains an interpretation of Wisdom as somehow divine and quasi-hypostatic, though not a person.[1] There are no adequate reasons for equating this principle with the Logos, the second hypostasis, as was done in Arian and anti-Arian patristic exegesis. Nevertheless, this principle is *with* God and is prior to the world. " The Lord possessed me in the beginning of his way, before his works of old ", viii. 22, it is therefore co-eternal with God (" I was set up from everlasting, from the beginning, or ever the earth was ", viii. 23, *et seq.*) Wisdom belongs to God " in the beginning of his way ", as " a wise master-workman ", and is his joy ; its delights are to be with the sons of men (30–31). We see

[1] " Wisdom is personal, but not a person." (Drummond : *A New Commentary on Holy Scripture*, II, 70).

a similar conception of the Wisdom of God in Job xxviii. 20–27. Proverbs, Ch. ix. 1–4, also speaks of Wisdom in this personified way, though this text seems to have a double meaning.

We find an ontological interpretation of Wisdom in the two pseudepigrapha, the Wisdom of Solomon and the Wisdom of Jesus Ben-Sirach (Ecclesiasticus). These together form a sort of metaphysical commentary on Proverbs. In the Wisdom of Solomon, in addition to i. 5, 8, ch. vii. is of fundamental significance. It treats of Wisdom, the master-workman of all, $\dot{\eta}$ $\tau\hat{\omega}\nu$ $\pi\alpha\nu\tau\omega\nu$ $\tau\epsilon\chi\nu\dot{\eta}\tau\eta s$, as also of the " spirit of Wisdom ". She is the " breath of the power of God, a pure influence flowing from the glory of the Almighty " $\tau\hat{\eta}s$ $\tau\hat{o}\nu$ $\pi\alpha\nu\tau\sigma\kappa\rho\hat{a}\tau\sigma\rho\sigma s$ $\delta\sigma\xi\eta s$. She is the " brightness of the everlasting light, the unspotted mirror of the power of God ($\tau\hat{o}\nu$ $\Theta\epsilon\sigma\hat{\upsilon}$ $\dot{\epsilon}\nu\epsilon\rho\gamma\epsilon\dot{\iota}\alpha s$) and the image of his goodness ". " She is conversant with God ", and is " privy to the mysteries of the knowledge of God ". By Wisdom the Lord has made man ($\tau\hat{\eta}$ $\sigma\sigma\phi\dot{\iota}\alpha$ $\sigma\sigma\upsilon$ $\kappa\alpha\tau\alpha\sigma\kappa\epsilon\nu\dot{\alpha}\sigma\alpha s$ $\dot{\alpha}\nu\Theta\rho\omega\pi\sigma\nu$). Wisdom " knows thy works for it was present with thee, when thou didst create the world ". Chapters x.–xii. represent Wisdom not only as the power which was present before the world came into being, but as a power which continually protects and preserves it.

Wisdom is portrayed in the same way in Ecclesiasticus. Chapters i. and xxiv. sing the praises of Sophia : (αἴνεσις Σοφίας)—" All wisdom cometh from the Lord, and is with him for ever " (i. 1), " I came out of the mouth of the most high, and covered the earth as a cloud " (xxiv. 3). Without going into detail we may say that the striking figure which conveys this teaching on Wisdom obviously does not admit of being interpreted in the sense of quality or attribute, for this would destroy the figure itself. But here we should notice yet another point. Though we must disregard the obviously inadmissible interpretation of Wisdom as the Second Hypostasis, or the Logos,[1] yet we must at the same time recognize that the principle of Wisdom has never received satisfactory theological interpretation or application, so that even to-day it is overlooked by theology and only succeeds in creating misunderstanding. It is impossible, however, that this should always remain the case.

A few words now as to the manner in which the conception of Wisdom is applied in the New

---

[1] The Arian interpretation was based upon the phrase " God created ἔκτισα, Wisdom ". This is, however, more accurately rendered now as ἐκτήσατο " had ", " possessed ", " formed me " (22). It is true that verse 24 reads " gives birth to me ", γεννᾷ με (" I was brought forth " or " I was fashioned "). But if we compare this expression with v. 22 we shall see that it cannot be regarded as having a dogmatic reference to the Son.

Testament. We will not consider here the comparatively numerous texts in which Wisdom is
definitely to be understood as a property (2 Peter
iii. 15 ; Rom. xi. 33 ; 1 Cor. i. 17, 20–30 ; Eph.
i. 8, 17 ; iii. 10 ; Col. i. 9, 28 ; xi. 3 ; iii.
16 ; Rev. v. 12 ; vii. 12). We have a passage
(1 Cor. i. 24), where this principle is applied
Christologically (cp. Luke xi. 49), but we also
observe that it is used without any relation to
Christology in Matt. xi. 19, and Luke vii. 35.
But even this Christological adaptation should
be understood in the light of, and in connection
with, Old Testament sophiology (see below).

We thus observe in biblical theology side by
side with a revelation of the personal being of God,
a doctrine of Divine Wisdom either in God or
with God. But alongside the idea of Wisdom
we see in the Old Testament also yet another
striking figure, namely, that of the Shekinah, the
Glory of God, in the midst of which God manifests himself. We meet this for the first time in
Exodus xvi. 7–10 : " Ye shall see the glory of the
Lord . . . and, behold, the glory of the Lord
appeared in the cloud." (v. Lev. ix. 16, 23 ;
Numbers xiv. 10 ; xvi. 19, 42 ; xx. 6.) The
Glory of the Lord fills the tabernacle like a cloud
(Exodus xl. 34–35, cp. Numbers ix. 15–23,;
similarly Solomon's Temple (1 Kings viii. 10–11 ;

2 Chron. v. 13–14). God's appearance to Moses on Mount Sinai has, of course, a very special significance. This also took place in a cloud of Glory. Exod. xxiv. 16–18, and especially xxxiii. 18–23, describe how Moses, in fulfilment of his desire, was allowed to behold the Glory of God, and in this instance a vision of the Glory of God is contrasted with a vision of the " face " of the Lord. The vision of Glory itself is described thus : " And the Lord descended in the cloud, and stood with him there, and proclaimed the name of the Lord. And the Lord passed by before him, and proclaimed, ' The Lord, the Lord, a God full of compassion and gracious, slow to anger, and plenteous in mercy and truth (xxxiv. 5–6).' " In this passage (xxxiii. 22–23) two comparisons are drawn simultaneously. On the one hand the Glory is contrasted with the Face of God, to wit, his hypostatic revelation ; on the other hand, the manifestation of Glory is identified with the manifestation of God himself, which is shown by the proclamation of God's Name.

God's manifestation of himself to Moses may be compared with his manifestation to another great prophet, Elijah, who subsequently, together with Moses, was a witness of Christ's glory on the Mount of Transfiguration. God manifests himself to Elijah on Mount Horeb, no longer in a

cloud, but in a " still small voice " (1 Kings xix.
12). Then follows the great prophet Isaiah, who
sees a vision of the Lord on his throne : " and his
train filled the temple " (Isaiah vi.) . . . τῆς δοξῆς.
Finally we get the most monumental figure of
God's glory in the vision of Ezekiel (i–ii.),
who speaks of his vision of glory, as something
sensibly perceptible taking place in a definite
place and at a definite time, as something which
moves, comes nearer or withdraws : iii. 12–13 ;
viii. 4 ; ix. 3 ; xi. 22–23 ; xl. 2–5. At present
there is no need for us to analyse the particular
details of the appearance of Ezekiel's chariot in
all its complexity. It is an " image of the Glory
of God ".

If we compare all these visible manifestations
of the Glory of God we are inevitably led to ask,
what does it mean in its relation to God ? In
this case, indeed, we are not faced with the
temptation—which, as a matter of history, has
been felt in relation to Wisdom—to interpret this
Glory as either a created principle or a " property " of God. The glory of God in these
instances is obviously intended to represent a
divine principle. Though it differs from God's
personal being, yet it is inseparably bound up with
it : it is not God, but Divinity.

The same thing could be said about Glory as has

already been said about Wisdom, namely, that this conception has not only failed to receive any theological interpretation, but seems to have been completely passed over in dogmatics. The following tentative conclusion can be drawn on the basis of the comparisons made above. God has, or possesses, or is characterized by, Glory and Wisdom, which cannot be separated from him since they represent his dynamic self-revelation in creative action, and also in his own life. Moreover, it should be added that the Face of God, which remains hidden in the Old Testament is in the New Testament unveiled in its tri-personal nature. Hence we must conclude that the divine " substances " in question also belong to the Holy Trinity, for the sacred text gives us no grounds for limiting them to any one particular Person of the Holy Trinity—for example, to the Father or to the Son.[1]

What then is the relation between the dogmatic conception of Divine substance or nature ($o\dot{v}\sigma\acute{\iota}a$ or $\phi\acute{v}\sigma\iota s$) and the figurative revelations of the Bible bearing on the one hand on Wisdom ($\Sigma o\phi\acute{\iota}a$) and on the other on Glory ? Is there any ground for distinguishing and contrasting them ? In the

---

[1] The Arians and the anti-Arians who attempted to equate Wisdom with the Son, by their very attempt deny Wisdom both to the Father and to the Holy Spirit. The misunderstandings which arise from 1 Cor. i. 24 will be considered later on.

first place is there any reason for differentiating between Wisdom and Glory, as two distinct principles within the Godhead in its self-revelation, or its
revelation to creation respectively? There is no
doubt whatever that they do differ from each other
as two distinct aspects of the Godhead in its revelation: Wisdom, the first, concerns its content; Glory,
the second, its manifestation. Nevertheless, these
two distinct aspects can in no way be separated from
each other or replaced by one another, as two principles within the Godhead. This would contradict the truth of monotheism, for the one
personal God possesses but one Godhead, which
is expressed at once in Wisdom and Glory. The
fact of there being two figures does not make
two Godheads, however much these figures may
differ from each other. This doubling of the
figures is due to their peculiar nature, though
this does not in any way minimize the fact that
they are identical in substance. The Holy Bible,
however, is not concerned with systematic theology. It presents us with its similitudes in the
form of theological raw material, so to speak.
It is the task of biblical theology to understand
and to compare these similitudes.

Let us consider next what sort of relationship
can exist between the abstract Aristotelian οὐσια
or substance, the principle of consubstantiality

within the Holy Trinity (according to the recognized dogmatic definition), and the Wisdom and Glory which we find in the Bible. Perhaps, it may be said, there is no relationship between them (and as a matter of fact, in actual practice, theology has so far tacitly answered the question in precisely this way, for it has failed to observe the existence of any relationship at all). It is enough, however, to state this question directly to realize how impossible is such a solution. The denial of the existence of any connection between ousia on the one hand, and Wisdom-Glory on the other, undoubtedly creates a dualism in the Godhead. If ousia differs radically from the concrete figures which depict the life of the Godhead in Wisdom and Glory, then it becomes an empty, abstract, metaphysical schema. Monotheism, therefore, necessarily postulates the identity of the two principles—the dogmatic and the biblical. In a certain sense, which will be shortly defined, ousia stands precisely for Wisdom and Glory, " even his eternal Power and Godhead " (Rom. i. 20).[1]

---

[1] We see an analogy in the history of dogma when the Eastern Church accepted the teaching of St. Gregory of Palama (fourteenth century) which regards the Godhead as a Divine Ousia possessing energies ἐνέργειαι. This teaching regards the transcendent ousia and the multiform energies which serve to reveal it as equivalent, in spite of the differences between them. We have a similar " equivalence in difference " in the case of ousia, on the one hand, and Wisdom and Glory, on the other.

It is possible, of course, for the sake of simplicity in terminology, to fuse this triad of definitions, ousia—Sophia—Glory, and express its significance by any one of the three terms at random. But the actual history of dogmatic thought is hostile to such terminological anarchy, for every one of these expressions is associated with a definite shade of meaning. In practice, therefore, we should not restrict the circle of sophiological problems to the single term ousia. Such a procedure would be useless when we come to consider the place occupied in the history of dogma by this particular dogmatic precision. On the contrary it seems much more natural to link up the problems of our own time with the term " Sophia " (further amplified by the term " Glory "). Yet still, using an abridged and simplified terminology, we can say : the Divinity in God constitutes the Divine Sophia (or Glory), while at the same time we assume that it is also the ousia : Ousia=Sophia=Glory.

We are next faced with the question of how to conceive of the Godhead in reference to its hypostatic aspect. The tri-hypostatic God possesses, indeed, but one Godhead, Sophia ; possesses it in such a way that at the same time it belongs to each of the Persons, in accordance with the properties distinguishing each of these Persons (just in the same way as each one possesses the one common ousia).[1] Ousia-Sophia is distinct from the Hypostases, though it cannot exist apart from them and is eternally hypostatized in them. Thus Sophia is distinguished by the capacity of belonging to the Hypostasis, of being included, that is, in the hypostatic being, which nevertheless appears to be quite compatible with its own un-hypostatic nature. God is Spirit, and it is an attribute of spirit to possess an hypostasis which abides in its own nature, or to be the subject of its own nature, which is a unity of predicates, in such a way that their mutual relationship and connection expresses the life of the spirit. But this very life in itself takes for granted the fact that the nature of spirit is not a thing, but a living principle, even though it is not personal. Ousia-Sophia is the life of an hypostatic spirit, though not itself hypostatic.

But what is it that permeates the life of the God-head? In other words, what *is* God? God is Love—not love in the sense of a quality or a property peculiar to God—but as the very substance and vigour of his life. The tri-hypostatic union of the Godhead is a mutual love, in which each of the Hypostases, by a timeless act of self-giving in

[1] cf. Augustine, *de Trin.*, I, VII, c. I–III: Ergo et Pater ipse Sapientia est. . . . Unde et Pater et Filius simul una Sapientia est, quia una essentia. . . .

love, reveals itself in both the others. However,
the divine Hypostases alone do not constitute the
only personal centres of this love, for Ousia-
Sophia likewise belongs to the realm of God's
Love. It is loved by the Holy Trinity as life and
revelation, in it the tri-une God loves himself.
But its own being in relation to the Divine Person
cannot be defined as no more than the mere fact
of being their common possession. On the contrary, it too is love, though love in a special and
un-hypostatic embodiment. Love is multiform :
the aspects of love in the Trinity vary in each of
the Persons. But besides that which is personal
there can be a love which is not.[1] All life in God,
in itself, is love. In this sense we can speak of
love in God not only in the mutual relationship of
the three Hypostases and in the relationship of
God to his Godhead, but in like manner in the
love of the Godhead for God. Thus if God loves
Sophia, Sophia also loves God. Apart from this
the tri-hypostatic relation between God and his
ousia is inconceivable.

[1] A wide range of texts from the Bible, bearing on the love of nature
for its Creator (Ps. 19, 1–5, Ps. 148) ; the love of the Church for
Christ (Eph. iv. 11 ; v. 32 ; Revel. xxi. 9 ; xxii. 17), and others ;
and similarly a great number of Orthodox liturgical texts speak of the
existence of such an un-hypostatic, passive form of love. Apart from
such an interpretation all these expressions lose their whole significance and become rhetorical metaphors. The general meaning of
these texts is that nature praises God, that is, loves the Creator with a
special non-hypostatic love.

To sum up, the nature of God (which is in fact Sophia) is a living and, therefore, loving substance, ground and " principle ". But, it might be said, does this not lead to the conception of a " fourth hypostasis " ? The reply is " certainly not " ; for this principle in itself is non-hypostatic, though capable of being hypostatized, in a given Hypostasis, and thereby constituting its life. But, it might still be urged, would this not result in " another God ", a sort of totally " other " Divine principle within God ? Again we reply, no ; for no one has ever attempted to maintain such an idea in connection with the Divine ousia in its relation to the hypostases [1] while the very conception of ousia itself is but that of Sophia. less fully developed. The whole strength of the dogma of the Holy Trinity lies in this insistence on the one life and one substance of the Divine tri-unity, as well as on their mutual identity : God possesses the Godhead, or he *is* the Godhead, is Ousia, Sophia. This does not imply that the three Persons own in common, and separately make use of, a certain common substance—on the basis, so to speak, of collective ownership.

[1] The teaching of Gilbert de la Porrée, which was condemned by the Council of Rheims in 1147, contained the idea that the nature of the Godhead constitutes a fourth term within the Trinity, which is thus rather *quaternitas*. The Council very justly proclaimed that *Divinitas sit Deus et Deus Divinitas*. [*See* St. Bernard, *in Cantica, Sermo* LXXX. Tr.]

This would lead to tritheism, not trinitarianism. The living tri-unity of the Holy Trinity is founded on a single principle of self-revelation with one life in common, though in three distinct Persons. The Holy Trinity has one ousia, not three, or three-thirds of an ousia divided up between the three Persons. It likewise possesses one Wisdom, not three, one Glory, not three. Thus of its own accord falls to the ground the first misconception which arises on the very threshold of sophiology.

CHAPTER II

THE DIVINE SOPHIA AND THE PERSONS
OF THE HOLY TRINITY

THE DIVINE SOPHIA AND THE PERSONS OF THE HOLY TRINITY

THE Holy Trinity is consubstantial and in-divisible. The three Persons of the Holy Trinity have one life in common, that is, one ousia, one Sophia. Nevertheless this *unity* of divine life co-exists with the fact that the life of each of the Hypostases in the divine Ousia-Sophia is determined in accordance with its own personal character, or specific hypostatic features. One and the same Sophia is possessed *in a different way* by the Father, the Son, and the Holy Spirit, and this threefold " otherness " is reflected in our definition of Sophia. We should learn to think of the divine Sophia as at the same time threefold and one. The divine tri-unity is mirrored in her with all its characteristics. There is, however, a difference to be observed in logical emphasis when interpreting on the one hand the *tri*-unity of the *three* Hypostases, and on the other the tri-*unity* of the single divine Sophia. In the first case we are contemplating the personal Hypostases of the Holy Trinity, which differ from one another— *three* which are one ; in the second instance, there is only the one substance, whose being is determined in a threefold manner. The tri-unity of the Hypostases is reflected in the threefold modality of the one Ousia-Sophia of the Godhead.

Let us now consider in more detail this threefold character of the divine Sophia. In the process we shall discover that this threefold character which arises from the fact that the divine Sophia belongs to all three Hypostases, is a basic principle. Now there is a curious sort of prejudice in regard to sophiology, to the effect that Sophia can be associated only with one Hypostasis, namely, that of the Son, an association which practically amounts to identification. This conclusion is based on an erroneous interpretation of 1 Cor. i. 24 (with which we shall deal later). The acceptance of such an interpretation would necessarily imply (as St. Augustine pointed out), that the Father himself is without Wisdom, as also is the Holy Spirit, who is the very " Spirit of Wisdom ". This is obviously absurd. The problem has been over-simplified at the cost of being confused. Unitarianism is thus introduced into sophiology, in place of the trinitarian principle.

In so far as Sophia is a counterpart of Ousia, she is akin to the whole of the Holy Trinity and to all its three Hypostases, both as separate Persons and in their mutual association.

In the first place, Wisdom belongs to the Father who is the " First Principle ", or the Hypostasis disclosed in the dyad of the two revealing Hypostases, that is, of the Son and of the Holy Spirit. The Father [1] represents the transcendental principle within the Holy Trinity, he who does not reveal himself but is revealed in so far as he is immanent in the other Hypostases which reveal him. He is, so to speak, the divine Subject, the subject which manifests itself in the predicate. He constitutes the divine Depth and Mystery. He represents, as it were, that speechless Silence which is pre-supposed by the Word. He is intelligence contemplating itself ($\nu\acute{o}\eta\sigma\iota\varsigma\ \tau\eta\varsigma\ \nu o\acute{\eta}\sigma\epsilon\omega\varsigma$)—even " before " the articulation of its thought. He is the Primal Will, the principle of all volition, the Fullness participated by all being. He comprises the Unity of all, and is prior to all distinction. He is the source of Beauty which must exist before beauty can come to be. He is Love, although this love is withheld within Himself and as yet unmanifested. He is the Father,

---

[1] See *The Comforter*, the epilogue : The Father (p. 406 and following). Compare also *Die Tragœdie der Philosophie*.

the source of being and of love, that love which
cannot but diffuse itself.

But this principle of transcendence does not
exist in the abstract, shut up within itself, as it
were, for it is inseparably united with the immanent (in a bond of love). The transcendent
constitutes the ground and source of the immanent, and the immanent cannot exist without a
point d'appui in the transcendent. In the personal
life of the Holy Trinity this corresponds to the
relationship which exists between the Hypostasis
who reveals himself and those which reveal him,
in their mutual association. The Holy Trinity
itself is a relationship of mutual self-revelation
(though not of causal " origin " in the sense of
emergence, as this is usually interpreted).

The Father begets the Word and abides in him
by the Holy Spirit who proceeds from the Father.
The Father is thus disclosed in this bi-hypostatic
unity, in the dyad of Son and Holy Spirit. In
this process the self-revelation of the Father is
absolutely complete, for the Father represents
the Transcendent in the Hypostases which reveal
him and which correspond to the immanent
principle in the Godhead. Within the Holy
Trinity itself there is no room for any undisclosed
mystery : " God is light and in him is no darkness
at all " (1 John i. 5). The Father does not keep

back in himself anything which has not already been manifested in the Son, and fulfilled in the Holy Spirit : " As the Father knoweth me, even so know I the Father " (John x. 15) says the Son of himself.   In a similar way it is said of the Spirit : " For the Spirit searcheth all things, yea, the deep things of God " (1 Cor. ii. 7 ; x. 11). Therefore the Father is Mystery abiding in itself, yet disclosed in the dyad of the Son and Spirit.

As regards the unity of the divine Ousia-Sophia it follows that the Father possesses her first of all in the tri-unity of the Holy Trinity and therefore in common with the Son and the Holy Spirit. While in his personal, hypostatic being, he possesses her as a *source* of revelation, as the mystery and depth of his hypostatic being, in a true sense as his own nature—*natura*—which has still to be manifest, and is to be disclosed in the Hypostases which reveal him.   In so far as the Father permits the revealing Hypostases to disclose her, the divine Sophia abides in the Father primarily as Ousia, the undisclosed depth of his nature.   But this primordial divine darkness is identical with that " light which no man can approach unto " (1 Tim. vi. 16) wherein God dwells.   For " God is light and in him is no darkness at all " (1 John i. 5).   Thus, the Hypostasis of the Father in

himself remains undisclosed, for he is only revealed in the other Hypostases by the power of
his self-denying sacrificial love.   And in the same
way his Ousia abides within him, unrevealed, in
the capacity of Sophia.   This relationship may be
expressed by the following formula : Sophia, so
far as the Hypostasis of the Father is concerned,
connotes predominantly Ousia—prior to its own
revelation as Sophia.

Now let us turn to the Second Hypostasis, that
of the Logos, and his relationship to the Father.
In the Logos we have an Hypostasis which
directly reveals the Father, the hypostatic Word
of the Father.   The general relationship existing
between him who speaks the Word of God and
the uttered Word itself has been sufficiently ex-
pounded in Holy Scripture and in theology.
The Son is the Word of the Father, the Image and
Radiance of his Glory, his revelation in the Word.
The Logos is the proper Hypostasis of the Word
in all the plenitude of the *ancient* meaning of that
term ;   namely, the Word-thought, Logos-logic,
Intelligence contemplating itself, both the thinker
and the thought, intelligence hypostatized.   Even
within the Hypostasis of the Word himself we can
distinguish the transcendent and the immanent
principles, the subject and the predicate, him
who speaks—and what is spoken : the hypo-

static Word itself which speaks and the Word of words spoken, or the content of the Word. This Word spoken constitutes part of the hypostatic life of the Logos in his Ousia. It is precisely this content of divine thought which is disclosed in the Hypostasis of the Word in the form of Sophia or the divine Wisdom. It is this content in particular which touches and embraces everything : " All things were made by him ; and without him was not any thing made that was made " (John i. 3). The universal nature of the Word is here expressed not only positively, but reinforced by the negation. How then can we contemplate this *all* understood as the Word of all words, as the content of divine Wisdom, of Ousia, manifested as Sophia ?

In the first place we must eliminate any *abstract* interpretation of the words of the Word. According to such abstract interpretation words are but powerless, lifeless symbols. They possess no vigour of being, for they are but " abstracted " from some other alogical type of being—from " objects ". It is quite obvious, however, that we cannot think of any alogical form of being, or of any being outside logic, which would at the same time be an object for, or stand towards the Logos himself as something given. The words of the Word in themselves possess reason and life. They are, as it were, certain intelligible essences, which can best be described as, like the Platonic *ideas*, ideal and real at the same time, and endowed with the power of life. *Everything* is included in the world of divine being, considered from the point of view of its divine content. It is in this sense that this all comprises the Truth of being and the being of Truth, of which the Word himself says : " I am the way, the truth, and the life " (John xiv. 6).

We should now adapt what we have said concerning the hypostatic nature of the Word to the definition of the divine Ousia-Sophia, in the aspect which it acquires in relation to the second Hypostasis. If the words of the Word about *everything* are not mere impotent abstractions, if they are light and life, *ens realissimum*, the divine ideas of all being, then this being is the divine Ousia, but Ousia disclosed and manifested as Sophia, the Wisdom of the divine world, the ideal ground of each distinct specific being. If the Logos is usually described as the Image of the Father's Hypostasis, then Sophia as the Ousia in the Logos, represents the image of this Image, its objective self-revelation. She stands for the wisdom and the truth of all that is worthy of participating of divine being, namely, of *everything that exists*, since we cannot conceive of the existence of any source of being other than or opposed to the divine. All the manifold forms of being, as many as, having their own specific character, possess a word or an idea, are thereby included in the content of the divine Sophia. This content includes everything and nothing is excluded from it. It embraces within itself all and everything, all the fullness—the manifold Wisdom of God— πολυποίκιλος Σοφία τοῦ Θεοῦ (Eph. iii. 10).

It is equally important for us both to identify the Logos in his hypostatic being with this Wisdom, and to distinguish them from each other. Sophia does not exist apart from its connection with the Hypostasis of the Logos, without being hypostatized in him : equally the Hypostasis of the Logos does not exist apart from his connection with Sophia. Nevertheless, in spite of the indissolubility of their connection we must never lose sight of the distinction between the two.[1] The divine Wisdom consists not only of the Word which proceeds from the " lips of God ", and from " the lips " of the Logos, but also of the Word itself, the content possessing a life of its own. Within the divine Word the Word and its

---

[1] It is for this reason that the widespread opinion, based on an insufficient understanding of 1 Cor. i. 24, which simply identifies the hypostatic Logos with Sophia, conflicts radically with the main dogma of the Trinity, which *distinguishes* between Hypostasis and Ousia in God, and consequently also in the Logos, between the " uttered " Word or the hypostatic Word, and his content.

being cannot be separated or contrasted, for the Word contains words about that which exists, the one Word which embraces all, which is in all and concerns all—" For of him and through him, and to him are all things " (Rom. xi. 36). This refers not only to their creation, but also to their eternal pre-existence in the divine Sophia.

But if this is the case, if Sophia represents the objective principle which is mutually related to the hypostatic Logos, and is hypostatized in him, then we must establish in this particular case a mutual inter-relationship of *love*. This will be the love of the hypostatic Word for his Word of words—for Sophia. It is the love of the divine Hypostasis of the Logos for his own self-revelation, for his own divinity. At the same time this self-revelation constitutes the revelation of the Father in the Son.

The inner connection between the words of *the all* is also the inspiration of love, and not only " logical " association. Different aspects of love —both hypostatic and non-hypostatic—diffuse their radiance here. " Logic " in God does not stand for a cold, compulsory, inevitable link which binds things together (such a conception has its origin in the fallen world), but rather for a *reasonable* love, a special aspect, that is, of love.

And so it would be true to say in a certain sense

that the Logos is the Hypostasis of Wisdom, while Wisdom represents the self-determination of the Hypostasis of the Logos.   Or, to put it more concisely, the Logos in himself is hypostatic Wisdom as such—κατ' ἐξοχήν.   This is a favourite formula on the lips of the opponents of sophiology. Nevertheless if we want to understand it correctly its bearing must necessarily be restricted.   It can be accepted only in the affirmative, and by no means in a negative or exclusive sense.   If we affirm that the Logos *pre-eminently* represents hypostatic Wisdom, we do not mean to imply that the other Hypostases in the Holy Trinity are without Wisdom, and do not possess it at all.   Exactly the reverse is true, for Wisdom characterises all the three Hypostases, each in a special way, exactly as the divine Ousia is shared by all of them.   But the second Hypostasis has the property of being directed immediately towards the Logos, being in this sense identical with the Logos.   At the same time the Logos comprises the ideal content of Sophia, so as logically, that is ideally, to determine it.

But Sophia, the Wisdom of God, must also be determined in her relation to the Holy Spirit. For this, however, to be possible we must recognize as fully as may be the exact hypostatic place of the Holy Spirit within the Holy Trinity.   The third Hypostasis in the Holy Trinity unites the first and the second Hypostases, the Father with the Son. The Holy Spirit proceeds from the Father to the Son, either " through " (διὰ) the Son, according to the Eastern theologumenon, or through the Father " and " the Son, according to the Western theologumenon.[1] The Holy Spirit " proceeds " from the Father to the Son, as the hypostatic love of the Father, which " abides " in the Son, fulfilling his actuality and possession by the Father. In turn the Holy Spirit passes " through " the Son (ἐμμέσως), returning, as it were, to the Father in a mysterious cycle, as the answering hypostatic love of the Son. In this way the Holy Spirit achieves his own fulfilment as the Hypostasis of Love. He is Love within Love—the Holy Spirit within that tri-hypostatic Spirit which is God.

The Holy Spirit *together with* the Son discloses the Father in the divine Sophia. The Son *and* the Holy Spirit, together, inseparable and unconfused, realize the self-revelation of the Father in his nature. The Son cannot be separated from the Holy Spirit who abides in him ; similarly the Holy Spirit is united with the Logos " without confusion ". The Ousia being, as

[1] For a more extended treatment of the procession of the Holy Spirit see *The Comforter* (on God-manhood, Part II, ch. II, pp. 93–186).

Sophia, the self-revelation of the Father within the Holy Trinity, must, of necessity, be concomitantly a revelation of the Logos and of the Holy Spirit.

If we were prepared above conditionally to admit the truth of the formula that in a certain sense the Logos is equivalent to Sophia, we did so only with a particular and limited interpretation in mind. For the Logos, in whom the Holy Spirit abides only in a state of dyadic union (and *not* separated from the tri-unity of the Holy Trinity, to suggest which would be blasphemy !) constitutes Sophia only *with* the Holy Spirit. For this reason the Holy Spirit cannot be separated from Wisdom ; he both possesses and reveals her, in inseparable conjunction with the Son. Accordingly in a similar sense we can say that the Holy Spirit too *is* Wisdom, as has in fact been stated by certain fathers of the Church, such as St. Theophilus of Antioch [1] and St. Irenaeus, Bishop of Lyons. [2]

If the divine Sophia represents a mutual revelation of the Son and of the Holy Spirit, we must try to determine the relationship which exists between them. It is obvious that they neither repeat one another, nor merge together. In spite

[1] Ad. Autolicum 2, 10.
[2] Adv. haer. 4, 20.

of this fact, nevertheless, they are mutually identified in *one* self-revelation of the Holy Trinity,
in the one Holy Sophia. We find, however, that
a very similar statement is made in the trinitarian
dogma, which teaches that all the three Hypostases—the primary principle, the Father, with
the Son, and the Holy Spirit—possess one essence
and are thereby united in one common life,
although as Persons they are distinguished. In
the same sort of way should we draw the distinction between the two dyadic Hypostases in their
relation to the divine Sophia.

The Hypostasis of the Logos is the only one
which completely determines by himself the
content of Sophia, as of the ideal *all*, the all-
embracing " organism " of ideas, and the ideal
unity of them all. There is nothing, nor can
there exist anything, capable of being added to
this or taken from it—even through the third
Hypostasis. Here we should accept as our guid-
ing line the witness of the Incarnate Word about
himself and about the Holy Spirit. If in the Old
Testament the Holy Spirit is named as " the
Spirit of Wisdom ", we find that in the New
Testament he is described as the " Spirit of
Truth " (not, that is, as Wisdom or Truth as
such, but precisely as Spirit). " He will guide
you into all truth : for he shall not speak of him-

self ; but whatsoever he shall hear, that shall he
speak " (John xvi. 13). " He shall glorify me :
for he shall receive of mine, and shall shew it
unto you. All things that the Father hath are
mine : therefore said I, that he shall take of mine,
and shew it unto you " (xiv. 15). Such is the
transparency of the Holy Spirit so far as the Son is
concerned. By the power of this dyadic union
with the Holy Spirit our Lord promised to send
" another Comforter " from the Father, in whose
guise, as it were, he comes himself : " I will not
leave you comfortless : I will come to you "
(John xiv. 18).

We thus observe that if God's self-revelation in
Wisdom is to be defined as far as *content* is concerned as the words of the Word, the divine Word
in itself, then the participation of the Holy Spirit
in this di-une self-revelation relates not to the content, but to the special form and to the divine
Hypostases in which this content is manifested.
The Holy Spirit is the hypostatic love of the Father
for the Son, and of the Son for the Father. The
revelation of the Son is the divine Thought-Word,
the Logos of God concerning himself, " the image
and the radiance of the Father ", the Thought
which contemplates itself and the Word uttering
itself. The revelation of the Holy Spirit is
accomplished in the existent life of the hypostatic

Word, his living actuality for the Father, and thereby for the Holy Spirit himself. It is the hypostatic mutual response of the Father and the Son, their mutually jubilant love, whose exultation is justified by and based upon their mutual sacrificial denial of self, as begetting and begotten. And the Holy Spirit himself constitutes this " perfect joy ", the exultation of love between the Father and the son. The nature of love consists in giving all one possesses without withholding anything for oneself. The one who loves then receives everything for himself only through such a renunciation of self in the beloved. The Holy Spirit as hypostatic love is absolutely transparent in this relationship between the Father and the Son. In himself he constitutes this transparency, for he is Love. And as such the Holy Spirit represents the principle of the quickening spiritual reality within the Holy Trinity, the reality and the life of the Word of Truth. But the reality of Truth is Beauty, the "good " of Gen. i. 10, 12 ; the Word becomes adorned by beauty, because the Holy Spirit abides in him. The Holy Spirit who abides in the Son, manifests him to the Father in beauty, for he himself is " the beauty of the Lord " (Ps. xxvii. 4).

In the divine self-revelation, in the Ousia-Sophia, the "Spirit of Wisdom ", the Holy Spirit, represents the principle of reality. He transforms the world of ideas into a living and real essence, into a self-sufficient creation of God, the *ens realissimum*, into a world existing with the life of God. This constitutes the divine fiat in God himself in relation to his own being, the content of which is ideally spoken, and is determined, in the Word. But being in God is not, and cannot be, like being in things—a dead objectivity ; which incidentally, we only observe in our world because our powers of perception are so limited. No, the world of divine ideas, a world of divine realities, is a living thing, is in fact life itself. And the Holy Spirit is the breath of life " the breath from the mouth of God "[1].

This *life* of Truth in its own full transparency is *beauty*, which is the self-revelation of the Deity, the garment of God, as it were ; it is that divine Glory which the heavens declare (Ps. xix. 1). It is of this Glory, as an aspect of divine manifestation, or epiphany, that Holy Scripture speaks, as we have seen above. The self-revelation of Wisdom is equivalent to the self-revelation of Glory. Wisdom is the Glory of God and either expression could be used indiscriminately of divine self-revelation within the Godhead, for they

[1] In the writings of the fathers of the Church the Hypostasis of the Spirit is usually compared with the breath we take when we pronounce a word.

both refer to the same divine essence. Nevertheless
we prefer to describe this Glory as Sophia the
Wisdom of God—in other words to take it as
defined in its relationship to the second Hypostasis,
to the Logos, in so far as he gives it *content*, whereas
in Glory it is defined according to its being. But
just as when we consider the mode of the divine
self-revelation we must always remember that it
is effected conjointly by the Word and the Holy
Spirit, so here when we try to define it we must
in speaking of Wisdom imply Glory also : for
Wisdom is the matter of Glory, Glory the form of
Wisdom.

Thus we reach the conception of the self-revelation of the Godhead in the double figure of
Wisdom-Glory, which corresponds to the dyad of
the Word and of the Spirit. But, it may be said,
will not this line of thought lead, as it were, to a
splitting up of the one undivided Trinity into
two parts : the Father, who alone possesses the
divine Wisdom-Glory, and the two revealing
hypostases of the Son and of the Holy Spirit,
which manifest it in themselves ? Are we not
introducing in another form the error which we
have already refuted : namely that Wisdom in the
Holy Trinity can only belong to or be identified
with one of the Hypostases (as is generally
thought, with the second), and *not* be shared by

the other Hypostases? In other words, is not Wisdom made a basis of division within the Holy Trinity? In answer to which it may be observed that the ousia is one and undivided in the Holy Trinity and that the Holy Trinity itself, by a tri-une act, possesses it in common in its one life and that therefore in a similar way the Ousia-Sophia does not divide the Holy Trinity, but manifests it to itself. The basic postulate of this self-revelation consists in the fact of the fundamental distinction according to which we have the primary Hypostasis which is disclosed, the subject of revelation—the Father, who begets the Son and brings forth the Holy Spirit—and also the revealing Hypostases, the Son who is begotten of the Father and the Holy Spirit who proceeds from him. The content of this revelation is actually represented by the divine Sophia-Logos, as the manifested image of the divine Ousia. The di-unity of the two revealing Hypostases, the dyad of the Son and of the Holy Spirit, manifests the divine Sophia. In this sense we can say that their own self-revelation *is* Sophia. She can therefore be attributed to both the divine Hypostases of the Son and of the Spirit, who constitute her di-une subject. But at the same time we must retain the truth of the postulate that the dyad of the Son and of the Holy Spirit constitutes the revelation of the Father, so that their self-revelation is at the same time the revelation of the Father himself working in them and through them.   Hence Sophia belongs to the Father, for he is her initial and ultimate subject.   She represents the disclosure of his transcendence, of the silence and mystery of the Godhead, she is the Father manifesting himself through the Son and the Holy Spirit.

We thus come to the conclusion that the divine Sophia, as the self-revelation of Godhead, belongs to all three Persons of the Holy Trinity, both in their tri-unity, and in their separate being, and to each one in a way peculiar to himself.   She represents their self-revelation, and in this sense, she is their predicate.   But we must distinguish between the aspects of this predication.   The relation of Sophia to the second and to the third Persons of the Holy Trinity is immediate, in so far as she expresses the image of the hypostatic being of each.   The relation of Sophia to the Father is mediate through his relation to the other Hypostases, who disclose him to Sophia.

In summing up we can say that the entire Holy Trinity in its tri-unity " is Sophia ", just as all the three Hypostases are in their separateness.   But we should be clear in this connection what we mean by " *is* ".   The connecting word " is " here unites the tri-hypostatic subject with the predicate. The subject is an hypostasis which, according to its nature, possesses being and which discloses this being in its nature. Nevertheless this predicate, as the content of the subject's natural life, does not contain within itself the hypostasis as such, but only reveals him. And Sophia, in this sense, once more, is *not* an Hypostasis, but only a quality belonging to an Hypostasis, an attribute of hypostatic being. Therefore we should point out a very important peculiarity of such statements as the following : the Father, the Son, the Holy Spirit, or the Holy Trinity, " *is* " either Ousia or Sophia. Such a statement *cannot be reversed*. We cannot on the basis of the foregoing argument affirm the converse in which the place of the subject would be occupied by the Ousia-Sophia, and the place of the predicate by the Hypostases, for instance : " Ousia-Sophia is the Father, Son, etc." Such a statement would simply be untrue for it would contain the heresy of impersonalism as regards the Holy Trinity. It would equate with the Hypostases a principle which is in itself non-hypostatic although it belongs to the Hypostases. This is the ontological absurdity, the heresy, which characterizes all varieties of impersonal conceptions of the Holy Trinity (beginning with that of St.

Augustine, continued in those of Boehme and
Eckhardt, and culminating in those of Schelling
and Hegel).

Thus we have established the relationship
which exists between Sophia and the divine Ousia
and at the same time, through this, her relationship to the tri-une Hypostases. Each of these in
his specific way possesses Sophia and in this sense
is Sophia. The Father, *Deus absconditus*, possesses
her as his revelation in the Dyad of Hypostases
which reveals him. The Son possesses her as his
own revelation, which is fulfilled, and accomplished through the Holy Spirit. The Holy
Trinity possesses her as her tri-une subject, as it
exists in three different Hypostases ; and in its
tri-unity has her as its one Ousia[1] which in its
revelation is the divine Sophia.

---

[1] We must here draw attention to the meagre interest displayed in
the doctrine of the one Ousia in trinitarian theology. This accounts for
the absence of sophiology which would otherwise have been evoked by
this doctrine. It may even be said that the conception of Ousia has
remained in the lifeless scholastic form in which it was taken over from
Aristotle. It has merely indicated the *place* where future problems
would arise, and had been more of a theological symbol than a theological doctrine. Such a state of things could not last for ever, and
sophiology has come in our time to occupy this vacant place and
reveal the meaning of this symbol.

CHAPTER III

THE DIVINE AND THE CREATURELY SOPHIA

THE DIVINE AND THE CREATURELY SOPHIA[1]

THE tri-personal God has his own self-revelation. His nature, or ousia, constitutes his intrinsic Wisdom and Glory alike, which we accordingly unite under the one general term, Sophia. God not only *possesses* in Sophia the principle of his self-revelation, but it is this Sophia which *is* his eternal divine life, the sum and unity of all his attributes. And here we must once for all remove the common scholastic misunderstanding which makes of Wisdom no more than a particular " property " or quality, comprised in the definition of God, and therefore devoid of proper subsistence. If this were so, then, since Sophia is Ousia as revealed, the same consequence would follow for Ousia as such. It too would lose its place in the substantial being of the divine Spirit and become no more than a " quality ".

[1] *See* my work *The Light that Never Fades*: the chapters on creation, and *The Lamb of God*, ch. I : The Divine Sophia, Ch. II : The Creaturely Sophia, pp. 112–169.

88   THE WISDOM OF GOD

Such an interpretation obviously materially impairs the dogma of the Holy Trinity. It would imply that God is a Spirit without a nature and that the divine Hypostases are in fact devoid of Ousia. Their being would be confined to an abstract relationship of mutual self-abandonment, without any content of nature, a conception akin to the *Ich-Philosophie* of the elder Fichte.[1]

In opposition to this scholastic abstraction which can only lead to heresy in regard to the doctrine of the Trinity, we must insist on the full ontological reality of Ousia-Sophia. Here is no mere self-determination of the personal God, but Ousia, and therefore Sophia, exists for God and in God, as his subsistent divinity. Yet here is no " fourth hypostasis "; we do not transform the Holy Trinity into a quaternity but merely recognize precisely in the Ousia the divinity of God, a principle " other " than his hypostases. It is quite natural, of course, for discursive reason to hesitate when confronted with the necessity of drawing a distinction between the hypostatic and the essential, sophianic, being of the one self-sufficient divine Spirit. Such a distinction, however, is only a consequence of the trinitarian

---

[1] We can see a contrary error in the denial of personality in spirit, leaving it no more than nature devoid of personal consciousness of self. Such is the philosophy of the " unconscious " in Schopenhauer, Hartmann and Drews.

dogma, which is a doctrine not only of the hypostases of the Trinity, but also of the consubstantiality of their nature. No more will sound ontology, however, suffer us to reduce the essential nature of the Godhead to the shadowy existence of a logical abstraction.

We are here confronted with an apposition of two postulates, which is for abstract reason an antimony : 1. God has Ousia or Sophia, in a sense *is* his Ousia or Sophia—that is the thesis of its identity ; 2. Ousia or Sophia *exists* only in God, belongs to him, as the very ground of his being—that is the antithesis—distinction. Both affirmations are true : the Ousia or Sophia is the non-hypostatic essence, which yet cannot exist but in connection with the tri-hypostatic person of God. This antinomy may be somewhat elucidated by comparison with the relationship between spirit and body in man. Man's spirit cannot exist without the body, any more than the body can exist in isolation from the spirit. As such, the body is not merely an aggregate of bones and muscles belonging to the matter of the world ; it is more than mere matter. The body should be understood as a revelation of the spirit, of its likeness and of its life. Being informed by intelligence, it provides for human individuality its outward expression—it is, so to speak, an icon of the spirit which dwells in it. The body, as a living organism, manifests within itself the life of its spirit, and is its revelation, its creation and its " glory " (compare Phil. iii. 21). The body on being separated from the spirit, ceases to exist as a body, and becomes a corpse, mere matter ; " for dust thou art and unto dust shalt thou return " (Gen. iii. 19) ; yet equally, the spirit once separated from the body, the man, in the fullness of his being, no longer exists.

Man, the incarnate spirit, thus provides us with an obvious example of the antinomy involved in the correlation of hypostatic and non-hypostatic being. To what extent, then, may this analogy be applied to the mutual relationship between the tri-personal God and his Wisdom ? It is usual to define spirit in general, and the divine Spirit in particular, by the negative notion of *incorporeality* as a being without a body. This is to take for granted that the body is simply the principle directly opposed to spirit. For the purpose of making clearer what the divine Spirit is we even make use of a comparison with the angels, the bodiless spirits. The incorporeal nature of the angels, however, only marks the special place which they occupy in creation, and their ministry to men,[1] but in no way can it be taken to express

[1] *See* Bulgakov, *Jacob's Ladder* (on the Angels).

the nature of spirit as such. The angelic world of bodiless spirits should always be thought of in conjunction with the world of human spirits, associated with the body, and by nature revealing itself through this body.

The angels minister to the world of men. That is why they are described by contrast, as bodiless beings ; a description which at once assigns them a place in the hierarchy of being, and thereby denotes a limitation of their being. No such limitation can be ascribed to the divine Spirit, which has in the Wisdom and Glory identical with its essence the sufficient medium of its self-revelation. On the contrary it would appear that this self-revelation, described in Scripture under the striking figures of Wisdom and Glory, can with greater truth be compared with or interpreted as the real prototype or exemplar cause of man's self-revelation through the body. We know that the Scriptures frequently speak of God's " body " or at least of its separate parts or organs ; head, ears, eyes, hands, feet, for example. It is usual to interpret this only in the sense of an allegory or as inevitable anthropomorphism. But would it not be more exact to understand it ontologically, in the sense that the organs of the human body, being instruments for revealing the spirit, must themselves have a spiritual prototype in the fullness

of the divine life ?   In other words, the bodily
form of man corresponds to the formal aspect of
that divine Glory, which is itself the fullness of the
life of God.   Naturally this simile does not hold
good when the body has become " flesh " (in the
bad sense)—for it would be more exact to describe this state as a virtual denial of the body—
but only when the body remains obedient to the
spirit and transparent to it, so long as it is a
" spiritual body " (1 Cor. xv. 44).   The very
expression " spiritual body ", far from being a
contradiction in terms or a paradox, corresponds
to the prime exemplar of the body, which has its
prototype in the Wisdom and Glory of God.

Indeed we can pursue this analogy yet further.
We can actually draw a distinction within the
body between its " reasonable soul " ($\psi\upsilon\chi\acute{\eta}$ $\nu o\epsilon\rho\acute{a}$)
and the sensible body as such, in other words
between its form and matter, the principles representative respectively of the Logos and the Spirit,
of Reason and of Beauty.   Hence the body has a
two-fold determination, which corresponds to the
dyadic character of the self-revelation of God
through Wisdom and Glory in the second and
third hypostases.

Thus the essential Wisdom and Glory in God
possesses an ontological reality analogous to that
of a body informed by a reasonable soul in its

relation to the spirit incarnate in it. And
accordingly it can be compared to an absolute,
heavenly, spiritual body belonging to the divine
Spirit in all the fullness of its self-revelation.
There is reference to this fullness, πλήρωμα, in relation to the incarnate Word in the phrase " in him
dwelleth all the fulness of the Godhead bodily "
(Col. ii. 9). That inner self-revelation of God
which is described as fullness in reference to his
Wisdom and Glory, can also be defined as the
" world " of God in reference to the personal
life of the Deity itself. This life, obviously, cannot be without content ; on the contrary, it is
precisely by its fullness that it transcends all
definition. The simplicity of God's spiritual
essence is not mere uniformity, any more than the
divine unity excludes multiplicity. On the contrary simplicity precisely implies fullness, a fullness
in which all qualities meet in one. This unity
of all with all and in all is the ground of the
energy of love within the Godhead. As regards
its content Sophia as the " world " of God represents a " pan-organism " of the ideas of all in the
all, while the vital power of this organism is derived from the Holy Spirit. That, in effect, is
what the Godhead is for God.

But a question at once arises—can we as creatures presume to penetrate into the inner life of

the Deity itself and pronounce any sort of opinion on it ? Are not such attempts on our part merely the product of an insane daring and an impotent presumption ? Do not the prohibitions of the *via negationis*, the *docta ignorantia*, whose wisdom consists only in knowing that we know nothing, come nearer to the heart of the matter ? Such doubts are expressed in various quarters in relation to sophiology. Are they justified ?

Now it is true, of course, that the absolute God can never be comprehended by human reason. God transcends the world and man to such an extent that even the purely negative theology which denies all possibility of knowing anything about God, has nevertheless already gone too far in affirming so much as that. Even negation must make one positive assumption. Indeed, the only thing which would seem to meet the case would be the absence of any sort of thought or teaching about God, a form of agnosticism which would merge into practical atheism. God in his mercy, however, has not left us in the darkness of such agnosticism : he has given us a revelation concerning himself. He reveals himself to us both in his tri-personal being and in the simplicity of his deity, and only in virtue of such revelation dare we make any positive statement about God ; we not only may, we must.

The absolute God, who exists in himself, self-contained in his absoluteness, self-sufficing in his majesty, abandons this state and establishes in dependence upon his own absolute being a relative creaturely being. It is only in relation to this being that he can be called God.[1] Eternity lays the foundation for time, non-spatial for spatial beings, changelessness for becoming, while God abides " in the heavens " in his eternity and absoluteness. This state in which the absoluteness of the Absolute is combined with the relationship joining the world to God, the divine life in itself on the one hand with its manifestation in the created universe on the other, constitutes the ultimate antinomy for our reason and knowledge, a bound which we cannot pass. At this point the fiery sword bars the way to our reason, which can do no more than recognize the existence of this antinomy, accepting both its postulates as equally necessary, though by their very essence mutually exclusive. In practice this antinomy can be expressed for us in the following proposition : *the Absolute reveals itself to us as God*; and we learn to know God as such only on the basis of this his revelation of himself in his tri-personal being and in his Godhead, that is, the Glory and Wisdom of his essence.

---

[1] " The notion of God is a relative one." St. Basil the Great. *Deus est vox relativa.* Sir Isaac Newton.

Alongside of the divine and eternal world, there exists the world of creaturely being established by God in time. And God created it from " nothing ". What does this expression mean ? It marks in the first place the fact that there exists no other principle of creation outside of God or apart from God. This at once excludes that Manichean dualism, according to which there exists side by side with the true God some anti-god, who is the true source of the world of creatures. At the same time this affirmation also does away with the pagan materialism which assumes, in such mythological figures as that of Tiamat, the existence of prime matter, as it were, along with God. There can be no source of the world but God. This is as much as to say that the world has been established in its being by God, tnat it has been created by God by his own power and out of himself. Therefore the creature is distinct from the deity itself not in respect of the source of its being, but only in respect of the particular mode of its reception of that being.

But, meditating on the creation of the world from nothing, we can hardly help asking ourselves whether this " nothing " existed " before " creation and, as it were, on the other side of creation. We cannot imagine this " nothing " as in any way forming a limitation for God, neither can we think of it as a void, somehow " surrounding " God's being. " Nothing " means " no thing ", not " a thing " existing outside God. Hence, in order to *be*, " nothing " itself must originate in, must be established by God, who, according to an expression of Pseudo-Dionysius is (in this sense) the creator even of " nothing ". Indeed, non-being is itself a symptom or manifestation of the presence of being. In a certain sense the two are dialectically identifiable, as, for example, they are identified in Plato's Parmenides. " Nothing " here merely expresses the character of created being, with its relativity, incompleteness, *becoming*. Every such form of being must necessarily find its origin outside itself. Its emergence represents the filling of a void, of some deficiency of being, by some more positive, though still incomplete form of being. In this process of filling in, the non-being, the "nothing", itself acquires as it were a title to existence. In the act of emergence are present two poles : the positive source of being and the void of non-being, which is being replenished by its fullness. And in this sense fullness alone truly *exists*, while " nothing " is but the counter-part of this fullness in the state of deficiency. It is being in the process of becoming. Creatureliness as such consists in this fusion of being and nothingness, or of being and non-being. The

process of becoming lies at the very root of creatureliness—of its lack of power to gain existence
for itself, its dependence on the bestowal of that
power from above, in which consists the fact of
creation. This is the manifestation outside God
of the wealth of divine being, now enshrined in
creation and existing in dependence upon the
divine being.

If, then, the world does not possess in itself the
capacity to exist, but acquires it from God, we
may well inquire what is the relation between the
divine power sustaining the being of the world
and God's own inner life, his nature—Wisdom?

The first and most fundamental question which
we must ask is this : is the content of the life of the
world, or rather are the divine principles on
which it is based, something new for God himself, which was unknown to him prior to creation
and which was lacking in him, apart from his
relationship to creation? It is enough to raise
this question to be able to see the obvious answer.
For as soon as we admit that the principle of
creation is something *new* to God himself, we must
recognize a certain incompleteness in God without
creation. This inevitably forces us to the further
conclusion, that the creation of the world, is in
some sense, a sort of self-revelation for God himself. Let us make this assumption that with crea-

tion there emerges something new in God, which did not exist before. But this in its turn cuts at the very roots of God's absoluteness and self-sufficiency, and denies the fullness of divine life within him. We see, therefore, that such an affirmation leads to the theological absurdity and contradiction that the self-sufficient God creates the world in response to a certain need for fulfilment, and in the world discovers something new to himself.

It is obviously, then, essential for us to accept the opposite point of view. God creates the world, as it were, out of himself, out of the abundance of his own resources. Nothing new is introduced for God by the life of the world of creatures. That world only receives, according to the mode proper to it, the divine principle of life. Its being is only a reflection and a mirror of the world of God. We find this line of thought in the teaching of some of the Fathers of the Church. For them, God contained within himself before the creation of the world the divine prototypes, παραδείγματα, the destinies, προορισμοί of all creatures ; so that the world bears within it the image and, as it were, the reflection of the divine Prototype. We find such teaching even in those Fathers of the Church who in dealing with the subject of Wisdom, especially in their interpreta-

tion of Proverbs viii. 22, remained under the
influence of the difficulties raised by Arius, and
were thus apt to identify Wisdom simply with the
hypostasis of the Son. Yet in spite of this, in their
teaching on the creation of the world they affirm
the existence of the divine prototypes of creation,
in full accordance with the sophiological point of
view. Such, for example, is the teaching of St.
Athanasius.[1] The Pseudo-Dionysius quite definitely speaks of such prototypes,[2] so do St. John of
Damascus,[3] St. Maximus the Confessor and
St. Gregory of Nyssa, St. Augustine,[4] and perhaps with the greatest precision and directness,
St. Gregory Nazianzen.[5]

[1] *See* Bulgakov, *The Burning Bush*, excursus III.

[2] De divin. nom. c. 5, IX. Migne. Patr. Gr. t. 3, c. 824 : " The
prototypes exist in God as essential and complete ($\epsilon\dot{v}\iota\alpha\iota\omega s$) pre-existent
bases,which are described by theology as predestinations ($\pi\rho oo\rho\iota\sigma\mu o\dot{v}s$)."

[3] *In Defence of the Holy Icons against Gainsayers :* I, X ; III, XIX.
" The second aspect of the image is the thought which exists in God
in regard to that which he is to create, his eternal counsel, which is ever
the same, *for the Deity is immutable, and its counsel has no beginning.* . . .
For images and examples of all that shall be created by God are simply
his thought in him of these objects . . . in his counsel we see traced out
and represented what he has foreordained ; this is his thought of each
such object."

[4] Ang Tr. 1. in Joan. Migne. Patr. Lat. t. 34-35. c. 1387.

[5] Carmina Mystica. Mign. Patr. Gr. t. 37, c. 472.
" I ask : if to God we can never ascribe either inactivity or incompleteness, then whereupon was the supreme mind engaged during that
all eternity wherein he reigned over the void, while as yet he had not
made the world, and adorned it with forms ?
The object of his contemplation then was the adorable radiance of
his own goodness and intelligence, and the equal perfection of glory

What then are these eternal prototypes of
creation, which are recognized by the Fathers of
the Church as its divine foundation ? Although
the Fathers themselves do not describe them by
the name of the divine Sophia, nevertheless in
essence we have here, quite undoubtedly, the
divine world considered as the prototype of the
creaturely. Thus the doctrine of Sophia as the
prototype of creation finds ample support in the
tradition of the Church. If in the light of what
has been stated above we turn to Proverbs viii.
22–33, and the parallels in the pseudepigrapha
(see above ch. 1) it will not be difficult for us to
convince ourselves that here also the Wisdom of
God is represented precisely as a prototype of
creation existing with God prior to the creation
of the world. It is the delight in creation of God
the " cunning workman ". " And Wisdom was
with thee : which knoweth thy works, and was
present when thou madest the world " (Wisdom
of Solomon ix. 9). When God made the world

---

of all the thrice-radiant Godhead, no less truly so to himself in his
solitude than to those unto whom he has now revealed it.   *And
likewise that mind whence the world is begotten then dwelt in the depth
of his mind upon how he should give shape to that world which was
afterwards brought into being, and which even then was thus present to
God.*

For God has all things ever under his eye, both what is yet to be,
and what was, and is now. That division whereby one thing is
before another or after in time is imposed upon me ; but for God
all is fused into one, and held in the grasp of his Godhead."

" then did he see it and declare it (Wisdom) "
(Job xxviii. 27).

However we may in other respects interpret the
biblical teaching on Wisdom in relation to the
divine Hypostases, there is no doubt that it
includes this doctrine of the divine prototypes of
creation in God : by Wisdom God made the
world (cf. Ps. civ. 24). Usually these ideas are
rationalistically interpreted in the sense that God
created the world *wisely*, as if Wisdom were no
more than an attribute of God. The inadequacy
of such an interpretation is, however, obvious.
Wisdom is to be understood ontologically, not as
an abstract quality, but as the ever present power
of God, the divine essence, as the Godhead itself.
The former way of interpreting such passages as
Prov. viii. 22–31 was determined by the fact that
Wisdom was simply equated with the hypostatic
Logos, the creator of the world, through whom
" all things were made ; and without him was not
anything made that was made " (John i. 3, cf.
Rom. ii. 36). Such an interpretation, however,
proves too much, in effect making the Logos
alone of the Holy Trinity the creator of the world.
This is to contradict the irrefragable fact that the
creation of the world was the work of the whole
Holy Trinity. But, further, the usual formula
used by the Fathers appropriates the creation of

the world to the Father, working *through* the Word *by* the Holy Spirit, attributing to the latter an almost instrumental rôle. They are even compared to God's hands in the work of creation by St. Basil the Great among others.[1]

In what is revealed about creation it is emphasized that it has a " beginning ". " In the beginning God created the heaven and the earth " (Gen. i. 1), " The Lord possessed me in the beginning of his ways " (Prov. viii. 22). To this it is natural to add John i. 1 : " In the beginning was the Word." It is usual to interpret this " beginning " as a matter of temporal succession and to see no more in it than an indication of the order of sequence of events. This is especially strange in relation to John i. 1. If what has been argued above holds good, this " beginning " imports rather a divine principle of life, the essential wisdom of God. If we adopt this interpretation, then all these texts become evidence for a principle in God which gives rise to the world : God created the world by his divinity, by that Wisdom whereby he eternally reveals himself unto himself. It is

---

[1] St. Basil describes the Father as initiating (προκαταρκτική), the Son as sustaining (δημιουργική), the Holy Spirit as crowning (τελειωτική) the work of creation. St. John of Damascus speaks of the Father as the source and author of creation, the Son as the power of the Father predisposing creation, and the Holy Ghost as fulfilling all—" The Father did all by the Word, as it were by his hand, and creates nothing without him." cf. also : " The Word is God's will." Athan. Contra Arianos. II.

for this reason that the same revelation (John i. 1) includes the Word and the Holy Spirit.

In general, our position here is to maintain that God in his three Persons created the world on the *foundation* of the Wisdom common to the whole Trinity. This is the meaning which underlies the narrative of the creation of the world in six days (Gen. i. 3–31). We have then the following general scheme of creation : God creates by his Word, calling all things into existence by his creative *fiat*, " God said. . . ." We can distinguish here the Person of the Creator—God the Father ; " the Father Almighty, Maker of heaven and earth And of all things visible and invisible "; his creative word ; and its accomplishment. Certainly, the Word, which contains in itself every word of God concerning creation, and the Spirit, who brings all to fulfilment, are equally Persons in the Holy Trinity. It is quite obvious, however, from the text, that it is precisely the Father in person who initiates this act of God ; while the Son and the Holy Spirit participate in creation only in virtue of their self-determination in Sophia the words of the Word and the fulfilment of the Spirit. It is not the Word itself which speaks the creative word, but " God "—the Father,[1] who

[1] This non-hypostatic, sophianic character of the participation of the second and third hypostases in the creation of the world by the Father,

affirms it by his command " Let there be. . . ."
Although the tri-personal God creates the world
with each Person participating in accordance
with his personal character, nevertheless, the very
manner of this participation is differently determined for the different Persons of the Holy Trinity.
In creation the Father alone acts " hypostatically " in the name of God, while the Son and the
Spirit abandon themselves to the will of the
Father as his word and action. It is the Father
who speaks and not the Son, though the words
are those of the Word, as it is the Father who
creates and not the Spirit, though his is the
quickening power. Son and Spirit participate
in creation not hypostatically, so much as
sophianically, revealing themselves in Wisdom.
So it is said of the Son : " all things are made
by him ; and without him was not anything
made that was made " (John i. 3), and of the
Holy Spirit that by the breath of the Father's
mouth the strength of the heavens is established
(Ps. xxxiii. 6 ; and civ. 30 in the Slavonic
version).

We can, therefore, say that God the Father

is indirectly supported by the fact that, as distinct from the rest of
creation, man as a hypostatic spirit is created sharing in the likeness of
all three persons of the Holy Trinity. This is clear from the plural
used : " Let us make man in our image, after our likeness " (Gen.
i. 26).

creates the world by Sophia,[1] which is the revelation of the Son and of the Holy Spirit. At the
same time we should bear in mind that Sophia
does not exist in God independently of the divine
hypostases, but is eternally hypostatized in them.
Yet it is quite possible to draw a distinction within
the self-revelation of the Godhead to the effect
that this self-revelation may be predominantly
determined by reference either to the hypostases,
or to Sophia. In the one case we have a revelation predominantly hypostatic, in the other
sophianic. So that the creation of the world displays the following relationship : the hypostatic
Creator is the Father, who, being the principle of
procession in the Holy Trinity, creates the world
by an act of the whole Trinity in its unique
Wisdom. In this act the second and third hypostases participate not as separate Persons, but
somehow " kenotically ", concealing themselves
in the hypostasis of the Father, from whom initiates the will to create.

The divine Sophia, as the revelation of the
Logos, is the *all-embracing unity*, which contains
within itself all the fullness of the world of ideas.
But to the creature also God the Creator entrusts
this *all*, withholding nothing in himself and not
limiting the creature in any way : " *all* things

[1] *See* Bulgakov, *The Comforter.*

were made by him (the Word) " (John i. 3). In Sophia the fullness of the ideal forms contained in the Word is reflected in creation. This means that the species of created beings do not represent some new type of forms, devised by God, so to speak, *ad hoc*, but that they are based upon eternal, divine prototypes.[1] For this reason therefore the world of creatures also bears a " certain imprint "[2] of the world of God, in so far as it shares the fullness of the divine forms or ideas. This is clear from the fact that on accomplishing the work of creation God " rested from all his work " (Gen. ii. 1–3). This similitude implies the exhaustive fullness of creation, the twofold aspect of which as the creation of both " heaven and earth ", of the world of angels and the world of men does not affect the general postulate that the primary foundation of the world is rooted in divine Sophia.

God bestowed on the world at its creation not only the fullness of its ideal form as present to his own mind, but also the capacity to maintain its own distinct existence. This is the life which it derives from the Holy Spirit. " When thou

[1] The Platonic doctrine of ideas represents one philosophical form of sophiology, which, however, finds no support in the revelation of the tri-personal God. cf. *The Light that Never Fades*.

[2] According to his favourite expression St. Athanasius compares the relationship between the created and the divine Wisdom (which in a one-sided manner he identifies only with the Logos) with " the tracing of the name of the King's son on every building of the town which his Father builds ". (Contra Ar. II, 49.)

lettest thy breath go forth, they shall be made.
When thou takest away their breath, they die "
(Ps. civ. 29, 30). The action of the Holy Spirit
consists in the direct or indirect application of the
creative *fiat* to the different aspects of creation,
" let the waters, let the earth, bring forth. . . ."
(Gen. i. 20, 24). The quickening activity of the
Holy Spirit bestows on creatures in general the
capacity to exist, prior to the emergence of their
specific forms : " The Spirit of God moved upon
the face of the waters " (Gen. i. 2), that is to say,
over prime matter, communicating the capacity
for existence to the *tohu-bohu* of the " void ". The
Holy Spirit who thus imparts to ideal forms their
reality represents the power of *Beauty* or the divine
Glory. The Father confers glory on creation
after the likeness of divine Glory. The divine
approval of creation is repeated as a sort of
ratification of the work of each " day "—starting
with the third : " and God saw that it was good "
(Gen. i. 10, 12, 18, 21, 25). This culminates in
the general approbation of everything created.
" And God saw everything that he had made and,
behold, it was very good " (v. 31). " His work
is worthy to be praised and had in honour "
(Ps. cxi. 3). This the Slavonic renders : " His
work is glory and beauty."

Thus God created the world by the Word and

by the Holy Spirit, as they are manifested in Wisdom. In this sense he created the world by Wisdom and after the image of Wisdom. That Wisdom, which is an eternal reality in God, also provides the foundation for the existence of the world of creatures. Once again here we may repeat the dogmatic assertion that the world is created out of "non-being" or " nothing ". Yet its capacity to exist, and its abiding reality, is not without some ground. This it finds precisely in the Wisdom of God. To admit this is to affirm, in a sense, the fundamentally divine character of the world, based upon this identity of the principle of divine Wisdom in God and in the creature. Wisdom in creation is ontologically identical with its prototype, the same Wisdom as it exists in God. The world exists in God : " For of him, and through him, and to him, are all things " (Rom. ii. 36). It exists by the power of his Godhead, even though it exists outside God. It is here that we find the boundary which separates Christianity from any kind of pantheism. In the latter the world is identical with God, and, therefore, strictly speaking neither the world nor God exists, but only a world which is a god in process of becoming. In the Christian conception on the other hand, the world belongs to God, for it is in God that it finds the foundation of its reality.

Nothing can exist outside God, as alien or exterior
to him. Nevertheless, as created from " nothing ", in this " nothing " the world finds its
" place ". God confers on a principle which
originates in himself an existence distinct from
his own. This is not pantheism, but pan-en-
theism.

The created world, then, is none other than the
creaturely Sophia, a principle of relative being,
in process of becoming, and in composition with
the non-being of " nothing "; this is what it means
when we say that *the world is created by God from
nothing.* Nevertheless, though the positive principle on which the world is based belongs to the
being of God, the world as such maintains its
existence and its identity, distinct from that of
God. Although its whole being depends upon
the divine power of the creaturely Sophia within
it, nevertheless the world is not God, but only
God's creature. There is no such ontological
necessity for the world as could constrain God
himself to create it for the sake of his own development or fulfilment ; such an idea would indeed
be pure pantheism. On the contrary God creates
the world in the freedom of his superabundant
love. The self-sufficiency of God's being is
completely realized in the tri-hypostatic life of the
consubstantial Deity ; nothing else can add to it

or give it further fulfilment. In this sense, that
is, for his own sake, God does not need the world.

Nevertheless the divine freedom which has
manifested itself in the creation of the world is
not something haphazard, nor some casual whim
of such a kind that the world might equally well
have been created or not. The reason for its
creation is to be found in a quite different, free,
" necessity "—the force of God's love overflowing
beyond the limits of its own being to found being
other than his own. On any other view God's
absoluteness would set a limit to the Absolute
itself. In the creation of the world any such
limitation is transcended by God's omnipotence.
Through the act of creation the Absolute descends
into the relative. That which does not exist is
brought into being by the omnipotence of the
Absolute, who is in fact the God who is Love.
The Absolute then abides not only within its own
absoluteness, but also outside itself, so that the
world finds in it a God. This diffusion of God's
love into creation is accomplished not in virtue of
any *natural* necessity (as Plotinus, for example,
thought). It is a *personal* creative act of God, his
voluntary self-abandonment in love *ad extra*. But
in creating the world by his omnipotence from
" nothing " God communicates to it something of
the vigour of his own being, and, in the divine

Sophia, unites the world with his own divine life. In so far as the creature is able to bear it, he communicates Sophia, the creaturely Sophia, to creation.

Already as far back as the time of Philo, and later during the Arian controversies, there had arisen the question of the need for some mediating principle between God and the world.[1] This problem remained unsolved during the period of Christological controversy. The necessity of some such mediation cannot be denied, wherever the distinction of the world from God is held together with its participation in his being. Nevertheless it is not the hypostasis of the Logos which can provide such a unifying principle between God and the world. It was this assumption which inevitably led to the subordinationism evident in the Christology of Tertullian and Origen, and, more particularly, of Arius. The principle we require is not to be sought in the Person of God at all, but in his Nature, considered first as his intimate self-revelation, and secondly as his revelation in the world. And here we have at once Sophia in both its aspects, divine and

---

[1] It was to meet this difficulty that St. Athanasius produced his doctrine of the two aspects of Wisdom, the divine and the created. He develops it in his polemic against the Arians, in particular in his exegesis of Prov. viii. 22. *See* Bulgakov *The Burning Bush*, excursus III.

creaturely. Sophia unites God with the world as the one common principle, the divine ground of creaturely existence. Remaining one, it exists in two modes, eternal and temporal, divine and creaturely. It is of the first importance for us to grasp both the unity and the " otherness " in this unique relation of the creature to its Creator.

The act of creation itself remains a mystery to the creature. It is a mystery which goes deeper than the being of the creature, to the production of existence from non-existence through the omnipotence of God. Nevertheless we can dimly discern the limitations of created being, since in as much as we ourselves belong to this world of creatures we come upon them in our inward and outward experience.[1] The fundamental mark of the created world is becoming,[2] emergence, development, fulfilment. As a process this involves succession, variety, limitations of space, restriction—all these are aspects of being in the state of becoming. But although this becoming constitutes development, it does not represent evolution from nothing, in the way that this is usually interpreted in theories of evolution, for *ex nihilo*

[1] *See* Bulgakov, *The Light that Never Fades*, the chapters on creatureliness.
[2] Vladimir Soloviev in this sense describes the world as " the Absolute in the state of becoming ".

nihil fit. On the contrary, this development represents the germination of the divine seeds of being in the soil of non-being, the actualization of divine prototypes, of the divine Sophia in the creaturely. Nevertheless the seed remains only a seed, and not the plant itself. The world of becoming must travel by the long road of the history of the universe, if it is ultimately to succeed in reflecting in itself the face of the divine Sophia, and be " transfigured " into it. The creaturely Sophia, which is the foundation of the being of the world, its entelechy, ἐντελέχεια (in Aristotelian language), is at present in a state of potentiality, δύναμις, while at the same time it is the principle of its actualization and finality. The world is created in all its fullness, and God " rested from his works " after creation. This fullness, however, only applies to the content of the world, as God intended it to be when he created it ; it is not true of the present state of the world. The world created from nothing, both is, and at the same time is not, the creaturely likeness of divine Sophia ; it only approximates to this likeness in the course of the world process.

It is possible to ask : Is not the creation of the world, as it were, a sort of duplication of the divine Sophia ? But the whole conception of correspondence is inapplicable to the relation between the eternal and becoming. Indeed, it is nearer the truth to speak of unity, even identity, as between the divine and the creaturely Sophia ; for there is nothing doubled in God. At the same time, however, and without equivocation, we can speak of the two different forms of Sophia in God and in the creature. They are distinguished on the one hand as the simple and simultaneous perfection of eternity, as against temporal becoming, and on the other divine, as against participated being. The identity and distinction, the unity and duality of Sophia in God and in creation, rest on the same foundation.

This *coincidentia oppositorum* finds its expression on this account in a relation of type and antitype, an identity in distinction, and distinction in identity. This is the primary and ultimate antinomy of sophiology. And this sophiological antinomy only serves to express the still deeper antinomy from which springs all theological thought and to which it inevitably returns : that of the identity and distinction of God and the Absolute. Absolute being, self-existent and self-sufficing, while maintaining all its absolute character, yet establishes as it were alongside or outside of itself a state of relative being, to which it stands as God. The Absolute is God, but God is not the Absolute in so far as the world relates

to him. We find this theological antinomy reflected in a whole series of paradoxical relation-
ships : God and the world, the divine and the
creaturely Sophia, the type and the antitype.[1]

We must now take the last step in our endeavour to define the relationship between type
and Prototype, between the creaturely and the
divine Sophia. The created world belongs to
man.[2] Man, created on the sixth day to have
dominion over the world (Gen. i. 26–27), is not
merely one among other creatures, he is the representative of all creation, including in himself all
its fullness, a microcosm, a world in little, according to the expression of the Fathers. Even the
angels, the incorporeal world, minister to man
and in so far as they participate in this human

---

[1] *See* Bulgakov, *The Light that Never Fades*, the chapters dealing
with positive and negative theology. In order to avoid misconcep-
tions let us remind the reader that an antinomy differs both from a
logical and a dialectical contradiction. An antinomy simultaneously
admits the truth of two contradictory, logically incompatible, but ontologically equally necessary assertions. An antinomy testifies to the
existence of a mystery beyond which the human reason cannot
penetrate. This mystery, nevertheless, is actualized and lived in
religious experience. All fundamental dogmatic definitions are of
this nature. It is futile to attempt to dispel or to remove an antinomy.
In a logical contradiction, however, exactly the opposite is the case.
Such a contradiction is always an indication of a mistake in reasoning
which should be detected and removed. Hegel's " dialectic " contradiction, for instance, is in no sense an antinomy. It only applies to
discursive reason, which is incapable of embracing contradictory
propositions, but retains all its rights in the order of logic, where
dialectic is the means of advance.

[2] *See* Bulgakov, *The Lamb of God* ch. I, 4; II, 3–4; *The Comforter*
ch. IV, a, b.

world, are dependent on it. In this sense we may say the world is humanity, which includes in itself the formality of all the rest. And for this reason too God's image in creation is the human form. This also agrees with the basic fact that man was created in *God's image* (Gen. i. 27). We should accept this revelation in its full force and significance.[1] This " image " is the *ens realissimum* in man, it establishes a true identity between the image and its Prototype, which involves not only the " divinity " of man on account of the image of God in him, but also a certain " humanity " of God. As St. Paul puts it, " We are the offspring of God " (Acts xvii. 28).

In the vision of Glory beheld by the prophet Ezekiel we find the following significant passage : " And above the firmament that was over their heads was the likeness of a throne, as the appearance of a sapphire stone : and upon the likeness of the throne was a likeness as the appearance of a *man* upon it above " (i. 26). This is precisely the similitude of heavenly manhood. We come

---

[1] In patristic writings we find the greatest measure of such an acceptance in St. John of Damascus (*In Defence of the Holy Icons*, III, XVII–XX) : " Every image is a revelation of knowledge concerning what lies hidden. . . . The first, natural, and unchangeable image of the invisible God is the Son of the Father. . . . And the Holy Spirit—the image of the Son. . . . The second type of image is God's thought of what he was about to create, his eternal counsel. . . . The third type of image is that which God created himself in his own likeness, to wit, man." (Migne, Patr. Gr. t. 96, 1339–41.)

across the same human image of God in Daniel's vision : vii. 9–13 : " and behold, there came with the clouds of heaven one like unto a Son of Man, and he came even to the ancient of days and they brought him near before him " (xiii.).[1] The New Testament likewise speaks of the heavenly man, chiefly in relation to Christ : " He that descended out of heaven even the Son of Man " (John iii. 13). " The first man is of the earth, earthy ; the second man is of heaven " (1 Cor. xv. 47). " The gift of grace of the one man, Jesus Christ " (Rom. v. 15). The Incarnation is closely connected with this heavenly or eternal manhood. There is something in man which is directly related to the essence of God. It is no one natural quality, but his whole humanity, which is the image of God. It has its own line of development, its own history, but it is already fixed and marked out in man, as a constant tendency at the very heart of his being. It lies within us, something as yet unrevealed, yet surely to be revealed, if only when " God shall be all in all " (1 Cor. xv. 28).

Divine Sophia as humanity or rather as a

---

[1] Instances of angels appearing in human form, which are at the same time theophanies, would also be applicable here. A very important example is that of the three men who appeared to Abraham, in which many see a manifestation of the Holy Trinity : cf. Rublev's celebrated Icon.

principle within humanity, is not as yet identical
with man. For man is an hypostasis, in which
alone humanity, human nature, exists. Thus
Sophia in itself does not as yet express the whole
of man, which necessarily requires a hypostasis.
This man receives at the time of his creation by
the breath of the spirit of God. This is his Ego,
in which, and through which alone his humanity
lives. But human nature already has the capacity for receiving an hypostasis, after the likeness of
its prototype the divine Sophia, which can never
exist without an hypostasis, but is eternally
hypostatized. The hypostasis of the Logos is (in
the special sense mentioned above) that proper
to the divine Sophia. We can say of the Logos
that he is the everlasting man, the human Prototype, as well as the Lamb slain " before the foundation of the world "—in other words, predestined
to become representative man on earth. The
Third Hypostasis does not in this way form an
hypostatic centre for heavenly mankind, God-
manhood. Yet it does actualize and manifest
God-manhood, as a reality in God, to the Son,
and through him to the Father also. In this sense
we can distinguish within the eternal God-manhood the Logos as the God-man, and the Holy
Spirit, as his divine humanity. In consequence
there is a difference in the relationship between

the Logos and God-manhood and that between the Holy Spirit and God-manhood. But the Son and the Holy Spirit together[1] constitute God-manhood, as the revelation of the Father in the Holy Trinity. The nature of this relationship between the second and third hypostases in regard to God-manhood, can also be considered as that of those principles in the Godhead, which in creaturely mankind are reflected in the relation between masculinity and femininity. God's image in man is not fully unfolded without the interrelation of these two principles (Gen. i. 27).

This same relation, since the Incarnation, is reflected in that between Christ and the Church. Human hypostases are reflections of the Logos, the Heavenly Man, the " new Adam ". But the Holy Spirit, since he abides in the Son, is also a prototype of human hypostases. Thus man, created in the image of God, has been created male and female. Husband and wife, though they differ as two different exemplifications of human nature, manifest in their unity the fullness of humanity and of the image of God enshrined in it. Their union is sealed by the dyad of the Son and of the Holy Spirit, which reveals the Father. They bear within themselves the power of pro-

[1] *See* Bulgakov *The Comforter*, the chapters on the Dyad of the Son and the Holy Spirit : similarly the epilogue *The Father*.

creation, the image of the unity of the tripersonal God, which is to be traced in the whole of mankind as such.

Finally, the image of God, enshrined in man, is inseparably bound up with his *likeness*. The two are related to each other as something *given*, implanted by God, and something *imposed* upon man, the task he is called upon to fulfil in his creative freedom. The realization of this task is a painful process full of temptations and demanding effort, but at the same time it is the royal road, an effort wherein man can imitate God. Nevertheless for limited creaturely being temptation is always possible. Hence Adam's fall and what is called Original Sin. But even in his fall man cannot destroy the image of God within him, he only obscures it. However, as soon as man fell the whole of created nature also fell into disorder, for it was all bound up with man. And the re-instatement of fallen man takes place only in God-manhood, in the Incarnation of the Word and the outpouring of the Holy Spirit.

THE INCARNATION

THE INCARNATION[1]

THERE is plain evidence of Scripture for the opinion that the descent of Christ into the world at his Incarnation was included in God's eternal counsel concerning the world, " ordained before the foundation of the world ". Christ is " the lamb without blemish and without spot : foreordained before the foundation of the world, but manifest in these last times " for us (1 Peter i. 20, cf. 1 Cor. ii. 7 ; Eph. i, 4–6, 9–10 ; iii. 9–11). The love of God did not stop short at the creation of the world, but determined his own descent into it in person. In view of the fall, the Incarnation, as it in fact took place, was obviously primarily an atonement. But its purpose extends beyond this to the complete divinization of the creation, and the union of things in heaven and things in earth under the headship of Christ.

---

[1] cf. Bulgakov, *The Lamb of God, A treatise on God-manhood*, **Part I**, Paris 1933. The sophiological Christology here exposed only in outline is there systematically developed.

What then is the ground of the Incarnation ? Is it an act of divine omnipotence comparable to the creation of the world *ex nihilo* ? Or does not the fact of the Incarnation itself suppose the presence in human nature of some inalienable characteristic in virtue of which the possibility of the Incarnation becomes comprehensible, no longer as the invasion of human nature by some *deus ex machina*, but, on the contrary, as the complete unfolding of its possibilities ? Evidently the latter explanation is preferable. The ground of the possibility of the Word being made man underlies the very creation of mankind, which seems in consequence to make ready to receive him.

In his creation man receives a wordless call to reach heaven. That is the task set before him, which, however, he cannot perform in his own strength, but only in the power of God. In view of the fact of the fall, this aspiration towards union with God took the form of the prophetic prediction of Emmanuel, the Redeemer (Job xix. 25–27). For this purpose it seems natural that the person sent by the Father into the world to become incarnate should be that of the Son ; for the Word is the Prototype *par excellence* of humankind (see above). The person who actually effects the incarnation of the Word, however, appears to be the Holy Ghost, sent down upon the Virgin Mary.

Only as the result of centuries of dogmatic development did the Church, in the Fourth General Council at Chalcedon, produce the fundamental dogma of the God-man and god-manhood ; though the latter expression is not, as a matter of fact, employed in the definition. According to this definition, there is in Christ but one person, existing in two natures, the divine and the human, and that the second Person of the Holy Trinity, the Word. It was long before theological thought could hit upon the distinction finally attained in this definition. Christological controversy found expression in the acute differences between the school of Alexandria and that of Antioch ; on the one hand the monophysites confused the two natures, supposing the human absorbed by the divine ; on the other, the diphysites dissolved them, dividing the one God-man into two persons. The solution sought for was found at Chalcedon, in this unity of person within the duality of natures, in the form not of a theological synthesis, but simply a dogmatic definition affirming thesis and antithesis together.

This fact gives particular prominence to one feature of the dogma. The relation of the two natures in Christ is there defined not positively, but in a series of negations : *inconfuse, immutabiliter, indivise, inseparabiliter,* so that *salva proprietate utriusque, naturae . . . in unam personam atque substantiam concurrent.* For all its great and fundamental significance for Christian faith, it cannot be denied that this definition confronts theological thought with fresh difficulties. It is, in fact, thereby invited to go beyond the negations of Chalcedon to the affirmations there tacitly assumed. In other words, a proper comprehension of the definition demands a whole series of dogmatic postulates, which we must now expose.

According to the definition Christ, being " One altogether," perfect " as touching his Godhead " and " as touching his Manhood ", existing as one person in two natures, lives in both and, of course, with but a single life. Moreover the Manhood of the God-man is " enhypostatic " (ἐνυπόστατος) as Leontius of Byzantium expressed it, in the Word. That is, the divine person of the Word became that of a human nature as well. The suggestion was subsequently taken to be metaphysically possible, and sufficiently established. But how is it possible ? On what is it established ? Can human nature receive and make room for the divine person of the Word together with, or, more precisely, in the stead of the human person ? What does this imply ?

Human nature is elsewhere to be found only in the possession of a human person, and seems to admit of no other owner. From this we must infer that, since the person of the Word found it possible to live in human nature as well as in its own, therefore it is itself in some sense a human person too. It must be somehow co-natural not only with God, but also with Man, that is, with the God-man. In order to serve as a person to manhood, the divine person of the Word must itself be human or, more exactly, " co-human ". Its union with human nature will then appear not as doing violence to the latter, dissolving or anni-hilating it, but as corresponding to the original relation between them. While man, on his side, must be naturally capable of receiving and making room for a divine person in the stead of the human. In other words, man's original mode of being is theandric.

The incarnation thus appears to postulate, on its hypostatic side at least, some original analogy between divine and human personality, which yet does not overthrow all the essential difference between them. And this is found in the relation between type and Prototype. The personal spirit of man has its divine, uncreated origin from " the spirit of God " (Gen. ii. 7). It is a spark of the divine. Through his spirit, man is indeed made a partaker in the divine nature, and seen to be capable of divinization. This spirit once united with and animating a human nature " of a reasonable soul, and human flesh subsisting ", man already appears, by his composition and destiny alike, to be, in a true sense, theandric. And though his present state of sin obscures his memory of his heavenly birth, yet he has something in him which asks for God-manhood. Even before his coming the Christ who was to be was somehow contained in man. But man himself has no power to bring to pass the new birth in the spirit, which is " not of blood nor of the will of the flesh, but of God ".

If man, the creature, is by destiny thus theandric, the Word, on the other hand, who is his Prototype, is the everlasting God-man. It is in this sense that we take the position which lies at the base of all St. Paul's teaching on man. He speaks not of one, but of two : " The first man is of the earth, earthy : the second man is the Lord from heaven" (1 Cor. xv. 47–49; Jn. iii. 3), the " one man Jesus Christ " (Rom. v. 15). Thus it was possible for the person of the heavenly God-man, the Word, to become the person of a created human nature, and so realize its original

God-manhood. Since from all eternity the person of the Word was somehow human, it was possible for it, in becoming the person of a created human nature, to elevate without destroying it. We may even say that it was " natural " for the Word to take the place of the human personality of the human nature of Christ. And this is evidently possible because human personality in general is itself supernatural, and stands for the divine principle in the make-up of man. So the Word provides the person for the humanity of Christ also in his character as the second Adam. So, too, it was possible for human nature in Christ to receive and assume a divine Person in the quality of its own personality. And so we confess Christ to be perfect God and perfect Man, and the human compound in him to be maintained entire, for there is sufficient metaphysical ground for the possibility of the Word's descent into humanity. That spirit which in man is human, though derived from God, in Christ is the everlasting Word, the Spirit of God, the second Person of the Holy Trinity.

The Word, in assuming an animated body, assumes the whole nature of man ; σαρξ, St. Paul's equivalent for the phrase of the Councils : ἐκ ψυχῆς νοερᾶς καὶ σώματος; while maintaining his divine nature in indissoluble union with his person. What does this duality of natures in a single person here import? In the Chalcedonian definition their relation is defined only in negative terms: " inseparably and unconfusedly". But there must be some positive relation between them.[1]

The union of the two natures, the divine and the human, must be something more than the mere mechanical conjunction of two alien principles. That would be a metaphysical impossibility. And it would be wrong to call in divine omnipotence to justify what is contrary to nature as established by God himself in creating it. The omnipotence of God concerns the original creation of the world. In his providential government of it he maintains inviolate the nature which he gave it. The real basis of the union of the two natures in Christ seems to lie in their mutual relationship as two variant forms of divine and created Wisdom. It is conceivable only because manhood is the created form of divine Wisdom, which is simply God's nature revealing itself.

Consequently, along with the distinction be-

[1] In explication of this definition the Sixth General Council affirmed the existence in Christ of two parallel and concordant wills and energies, and thereby gave a less abstract idea of this positive relation.

tween the two natures of Christ, an analogy of
being is established. Here, in fact, we have the
affirmation implicitly contained in the negations
of Chalcedon. Apart from this analogy the
union of natures would be just such a metaphysical absurdity as the rationalist in fact supposes it to be. In the light of sophiology it will
cease to appear such : so that we may say that
the very dogma of Christology rests on sophiological foundations.

Obviously, in man, created Wisdom is ob-
scured by sin ; but Christ, the second Adam,
assumed a human nature exempt from sin, and
so adequate to its divine Prototype. But the very
possibility of God's taking human nature and
uniting it with his own, rests upon the essential
conformity between the two ; and that, in its
turn, upon the unity in diversity of Wisdom, in
God and in the created world. That diversity
can never abrogate this unity or analogy : this is
primary.

How then are we to conceive the one life of the
God-man in his two natures, " inseparable and
unconfused " ? Theology furnishes a general
notion which is applicable in the doctrine of
" kenosis " based upon the texts Phil. ii. 5, 6,
with 2 Cor. viii. 9, and Eph. ii. 10–17 ; v.7–8
So St. Cyril of Alexandria says : " The Word

willingly gave himself to be spent and of his own will stooped to our likeness, not ceasing to be what he is, but withal *while continuing God he did not disdain the measure of manhood . . . for wherein did he humble himself, if he abhorred the measure of manhood ?* " [1]

How are we to conceive this kenosis of the Word ? In the first place it is essential to realize that, contrary to the various kenotic theories of Protestantism, our Lord in his abasement never ceased to be God, the second Person of the Holy Trinity. At the same time, we understand his manhood to have been capable of so embodying his divine life, that he was in truth both Son of God and Son of Man. And between these two terms there must be some connection, an identity in distinction. This is found in God-manhood, that unity of eternal and created manhood which is Sophia, the Wisdom of God.

That the Son of God " came down from heaven " means that he confined that mode of existence which was his as heavenly Wisdom to the measure of its creaturely existence in man, to the end that he might then raise the creaturely up to the heavenly in the state of his glorification. He abandons " the glory he had . . . before the world was " (Jn. xvii. 5). That glory he gains

[1] Explanation of the 4th anathematism against Nestorius.

from the Father again when " the Son of man is glorified " (Jn. xiii. 31). Then only he says " All power is given unto me in heaven and in earth " (Matt. xxviii. 18). But this glory of his is itself, since it is his Divinity, divine Wisdom, and that in the Trinity means the Spirit revealing the Word. In the Incarnation the Word divests himself of this glory, and confines the life which is his in divine Wisdom within the measure of the created Wisdom in process of coming to be. *He remains in the nature of God, but devoid of his glory.* This sharing our nature and life, in which the kenosis of the Son consists, is a divine sacrifice, an incomprehensible wonder of the love of God for creation, " which things the angels desire to look into " (1 Pet. i. 12).

Together with this metaphysical kenosis we must take into account the further earthly, human kenosis involved in following the path of obedience even unto the death of the cross. The Godman lived his own life throughout along the line of this simultaneous self-abasement on two levels. Christ our Lord underwent all the limitations and infirmities of human life. He was subject to every human propensity which does not involve sin : he experienced hunger and thirst, exhaustion, grief, temptation—though without yielding to this last. He himself bore witness to his ignorance, or at least the limitation of his knowledge to the measure of human inference. He continually prayed to his Father in heaven as God, His mighty works, his miracles, he performed in the power of the Spirit and of prayer, showing himself in this " a prophet mighty in deed and word " [1]. He performed his ministry as Teacher and Prophet, imparting divine wisdom in human terms. And finally he fell into the hands of his human enemies and was betrayed to death.

He himself claimed to be the Son of God. Yet even this apprehension of his own Personality remained subject to the conditions of human growth. Of his childhood it is said that " the child grew and waxed strong in spirit, filled with wisdom : and the grace of God was upon him " (Luke ii. 40). " He increased in wisdom and stature, and in favour with God and man " (52). Times and seasons had their effect upon his life. It was throughout a life of obedient service, of *oboedientia activa et passiva*, till it led him to the agony of Gethsemane and to Golgotha.

The agony provides clear evidence at once of the reality of his human nature and of the depth of his self-abasement : Christ our Lord there subjects his human nature, " sorrowful even unto

---

[1] For this *see* Bulgakov, *On the Miracles of the Gospel*, A Christological Sketch. Paris, 1931.

death ", to the will of the Father, expressed within him as the voice of his own divine will. There, in his human nature the representative man feels the force of the sin of the whole world pressing upon him, the horror, for the one sinless being, of contact with sin, and of the justice of God outraged thereby. He took upon him the sin of the world in this way because he had already made himself one with all mankind. As the second Adam, his human nature is universal. Metaphysically, this was a consequence of the Incarnation. Spiritually, it was the work of compassionate love. Thus to endure the horror of sin and of the wrath of God directed against it, was already spiritually to have accomplished the redemption of mankind. But such a spiritual redemption alone was not enough ; there is the animal-bodily being of man to be taken into account as well. It was this which required his dreadful bodily sufferings and abandonment to death, with the final dereliction. The cry which resounded from the cross at the moment of his death, " It is finished " (Jn. xix. 30), marked the last depth of his abasement, and signified that it too was finished.[1] From that point his glorification takes its start.

[1] Actually the last act of this process was the preaching to the " spirits in prison ". We do not propose to dwell upon that here.

For a right understanding of the kenosis it is
essential to grasp the fact that the glorification of
Christ is at once his own achievement in virtue
of his obedience to the end, and an effect produced in him by the action of the Father, making
him worthy and capable of receiving it.   In the
former sense it is natural to take the series of texts
which refer to the Resurrection : Mt. xxviii. 6 ;
Luke xxiv. 34 ; Rom. viii. 34 ; 1 Cor. xv. 34 ;
in the latter sense the corresponding series : Acts
ii. 24, 32 ; iii. 15, 26 ; iv. 10 ; v. 30 ; x. 40 ;
xiii. 30, 32, 34, 37 ; xvii. 31 ; Rom. iv. 24 ; x. 9 ;
Col. ii. 12 ; 2 Cor. iv. 14 ; Gal. i. 17 ; Eph. i. 20 ;
ii. 5–6 ;   1 Thess. i. 10 (with which cf. 1 Pet.
i. 21).   The same distinction holds good for the
Ascension, on which we have, on the one hand :
Mt. xvi. 19 ; Luke xxiv. 50 ; and on the other :
Acts ii. 23 ; Eph. i. 19, 20.   In such passages
Christ is spoken of at once as rising, and raised by
the Father, ascending, and received up by the
Father.   This indicates that the Son's abandonment, in his kenosis, of his divine power and glory,
is prolonged even beyond the term of his earthly
ministry.   The grant of immortality to his glorified body and through him to the rest of mankind
at the resurrection, is likewise a new creative act
of God.   But it is not a new creation *ex nihilo*.   It
is merely the communication of the gift of immor-

tality to human nature, itself already created, and remaining at present, subject to death, but now rendered worthy and capable of receiving such a gift by the obedience which Christ freely offered his Father. " Jesus of Nazareth . . . God hath raised up, having loosed the pains of death : because it was not possible that he should be holden of it " (Acts ii. 22, 24).

And the final, conclusive stage of the kenosis extends even into the heavens, during those ten days between the Ascension and Pentecost, while the Son " prays " the Father to send the holy Spirit. It is then brought to an end only when the Son sends the Spirit from the Father. Christ, having left the world, henceforward sits as the God-man at the right hand of the Father in glory, until the time comes for his second and glorious coming, the Parousia.

What does this prolongation alike of the abasement and the exaltation of the God-man signify in regard to the hypostatic union of the two natures ? From our point of view, what is its bearing on the relation between the divine and the created Wisdom ? The distinction between the two natures persisted throughout the period of his earthly ministry. It was then necessary for his human nature to be brought into accord with the divine, with divine Wisdom. For he

took that nature in its created form and, as such,
impaired by the effects of sin, irrespective of his
personal sanctity and sinlessness and his virginal
conception exempt from original sin. The
actual condition of human nature by no means
reflected, as yet, its origin in Wisdom. Wisdom,
present in it in principle, had yet to be realized.
To put it in the ordinary language of Christology,
we may say that Christ's human nature retained
its own will, beside and below his divine will.
But for this human will to " follow " the divine
required a sustained endeavour, the supreme
effort of which was exerted in the prayer of the
victim contemplating his sacrifice in Gethsemane,
as witnessed by the cry : " not my will, but thine
be done " (Luke xxii. 42). " Thy " will is here
the one divine will, common to Father and Son
alike ; " my " will, distinguished from the
Father's by its very obedience, is the human will
of the God-man, bowing down to it. Christ our
Lord in his ministry fully and entirely actualized
all the potentiality of divine Wisdom even in his
human nature ; and it is with that in view that
he is called " Christ, the power of God and the
wisdom of God ".[1]

[1] This phrase (1 Cor. i. 24) can not be adduced as proof that Wisdom
is to be identified in particular with the second Person of the Trinity,
the Word, except through failing to notice that it refers not to the
Word but to Christ, that is, to the God-man in the sophianic unity
of his two natures.

In the substantial unity of the God-man created Wisdom is fully united and identified with the divine, yet without overthrowing the fundamental ontological distinction between the two natures ; the divine and the created. And to eternity they remain thus distinct, as the expression of the Incarnation and the resultant " composite " nature of the God-man. But in his state of glory they attain to that complete concord and interpenetration which is described in Eastern patristic literature as περιχώρησις, the *communicatio idiomatum*. This expresses the fullness and unity of that life, at once divine and human, which Christ now lives, and which is to be extended, in the final fulfilment, to the whole world, the whole of God-manhood. He himself, Christ our Lord, has raised humanity not merely to the degree of glory which it enjoyed before the Fall (Rom. iii. 23), but to a state of full divinization, theosis, whereby " God shall be all in all " (1 Cor. xv. 28). But this divinization, though evidently a result of the Incarnation and the work of the grace of God, yet cannot be without some ontological ground as well. Nothing can be divinized which has not the capacity and ontological aptitude to receive such a gift, which does not bear within itself some intimate exigency of such an end—in Aristotelian terms, its entelechy.

Divinization can result neither from some mechanical impulse from without, from some *Deus ex machina* ; nor from unnatural constraint.

The union of natures with its accompanying *communicatio idiomatum*, presupposes their original conformity. And this conformity we discover, in interpreting the two natures in Christ as the two forms of the one Wisdom of God ; those which it takes respectively in God and in creation.

Christ's created manhood is rendered transparent to his eternal manhood. From the God-man shines forth very God in his glory, the light of the everlasting Godhead, divine Wisdom. In him, indeed, for the first time the true idea of God-manhood, according to the conception of the Creator, is realized in its integrity, in the unshadowed clarity of its form. For God-manhood is the unity and complete concord of the divine and the created Wisdom, of God and his creation, in the person of the Word.

The dynamic aspect of this union of the two natures in Christ means that in him God is redeeming mankind, reconciling the world unto himself. Christ, the high priest, having entered into the heavenly places by his blood, pleads for our sins before the Father ; and this sacrifice of our redemption, offered out of time, and therefore for all time, finds its completion in the world

in the mystery of the Holy Eucharist. All the
humanity of Christ which has still to gain the
state of glory, all mankind which has ever lived,
is living, or has yet to live, remains united in a
dynamic unity with him, and so far constitutes
the Church, the body of Christ. And in this way
the withdrawal of Christ from the world at the
Ascension does not mean that he is separated
from it (Jn. xiv. 18, 19) ; it is quite compatible
with his continued connection with and abiding
presence in the world ; as, indeed, he himself
testifies : " All power is given unto me in heaven
and in earth " (Mt. xxviii. 17). This " and "
points to the link between heaven and earth, to
God-manhood, the unity of divine and created
Wisdom. This unity is realized in the progressive
penetration of the world by Wisdom, bringing it
gradually into conformity with its prototype in
Wisdom.

This process is accomplished in the continuance
in the world of that ministry of Christ which he
has already fulfilled in person in his life in the
world. It is a ministry at once prophetic, in the
Word, priestly, in the Sacraments, and regal, in
so far as Christ is crowned King of kings over all
the world. And its effect is to bring the world
into conformity with the divine plan for it, and
so to manifest it as the creaturely Sophia, the

Wisdom of God. Christ's connection with the
world, since the Ascension, is realized sacramentally, over and above his presence throughout the Church by the Holy Spirit (see below),
through his real presence in the holy Eucharist,
until the moment of his visible manifestation at
his second coming, in the Parousia.

The change of the holy gifts in the Eucharist
denotes the inclusion of the " elements " of this
world in the glorified body of Christ ; for that
body, though now taken from the world and
abiding " in the heavens " is no longer limited
by time and space and is capable of appearing
on every altar everywhere and at all times. This
glorified body answers to the human nature in
Christ, wholly divinized through its union with
the divine in the one person of the Word. Or, to
put it another way, it answers to the nature of
created Wisdom in the God-man, which belongs
to this created world, and stands for its glorification in Wisdom. The created world has still far
to go before the likeness of Wisdom appears in it ;
nevertheless, it bears that likeness hidden within
it ; while in the human nature of Christ, on the
other hand, this likeness is already absolutely
clear. Here, then, we have the identity and distinction of the two forms of created Wisdom at
once. As in the Incarnation the manifestation

in union of the two natures finds its foundation in their conformity in Wisdom as divine and as created ; so too the eucharistic change, μεταβολή, has its foundation in the *unity* of created nature, whether glorified or not. In becoming man Christ forged in his own body a link with the whole world of " flesh " ; it all now forms a potential extension of his body. The full significance of this link will be disclosed only at his second and glorious coming ; till then it is manifested sacramentally, and, to fleshly eyes, invisibly, in the Eucharist ; the primary effect of which, indeed, is to give us a personal union with Christ. But it also signifies the Eucharistic presence of Christ in the world.[1]

[1] *See* Bulgakov, *The Eucharistic Dogma*, in *Puit* (The Way).   Paris 1930.

PENTECOST AND GOD-MANHOOD

PENTECOST AND GOD-MANHOOD [1]

GOD'S self-revelation in the Holy Trinity is effected through the generation of the Son and procession of the Holy Spirit from the Father. Accordingly this self-revelation of the tri-une God is common to the Word and the Spirit alike, the two persons together disclosing the Father in one revelation—Sophia. Sophia reveals not the Logos, or Wisdom in person, alone, nor the Spirit, the personal Spirit of Wisdom, alone.

Its content belongs to the Word, its life and its being to the Spirit ; the former is Truth, as the latter is Beauty. Truth cannot exist isolated from Beauty ; nor Beauty outside of or parted from Truth. It is not the ideal world of thought, a lifeless abstraction alone, nor is it living reality devoid of all content and opaque to thought, which forms the content of such self-revelation. All thought without vigorous life is but dead and

[1] For the whole of this chapter *see* Bulgakov, *The Comforter*, Paris 1936, chapters IV-V.

schematic, while life devoid of its content of thought is blind, elemental. The Wisdom of God, as the self-revelation of Godhead, is live, vital thought, the word of the Word, upon whom the power of the Spirit abides.

Sophia is the heavenly Type of humanity or, in this sense, heavenly manhood itself. Hence this latter is also a common revelation of the Logos and Spirit, disclosing both persons together. According to Gen. i. 27, man is made in the image and likeness of God in a twofold embodiment, the masculine and feminine principles. These in themselves are not to be simply identified with sex and the sexual life, for this exhibits a sinful deterioration of the relations between these two principles, a clothing of human nature in " coats of skins ". This duality of the masculine and the feminine principles in man, which corresponds to the primacy of reason or thought in masculine, and of heart and feeling in feminine nature, does not divide human nature, though it inwardly diversifies it and thus goes to make up its fullness. The masculine and feminine principles in man subsist unconfusedly, while admitting of identification in some form of spiritual union. Yet they are at the same time inseparable not only in this sense, that either apart from the other does not possess human nature complete, but also in that the spirit of every human being combines elements of this dual principle, though of course in different ways and in different proportions. This feature of man as created in likeness to God undoubtedly finds its analogy in heavenly manhood, Sophia. Though here, of course, we can hardly apply in all rigour the earthly distinctions between the two principles present in man, yet no more can we rob of its force the analogy between type and Prototype. In particular, we must take into account these two complementary facts. On the one hand, the Logos assumed human nature precisely in its masculine, not in its feminine, or even androgynous, form. On the other hand, we have the Church, with the Virgin of course at its head, symbolized chiefly by feminine figures, as in the Song of Songs, in the Apocalypse, and in Ephesians.[1]

The world is created, as we saw above, by God the Father, who in the beginning, that is, in Sophia, the Son and Spirit concurring, spoke the creative word : " let there be " this or that. The Holy Spirit is dwelling unseen in the world, as its quickening force and reality. But he is

[1] Here it is natural to note the fact that in the Syrian writers of the fourth century, Afraat, for example, and in the old Syriac versions, we find the third Hypostasis spoken of frankly as feminine, the Syriac term for " spirit ", unlike the Greek and the Latin, being feminine.

present there not only thus to establish the world in its distinct existence and life, but also to elevate man, once inspired by himself, all the way to the heights of divine inspiration : "Who spake by the prophets." Under the old dispensation even before the descent of the Word the Spirit was sent to the world from God, from the Father, though, clearly, not in his person ; he was sent through his gifts, working as Wisdom on man in whom wisdom is immanent by his creation. The Old Testament knows various forms of the gifts of the Spirit, the Spirit of God : the spirit of battle, of kingship, of art, no less than the spirit of prophecy. This was already God-manhood in process of being accomplished under the old dispensation before the Incarnation. This out-pouring of gifts of the Spirit effected a union of natures between God and man, as it were, by anticipation, in the spiritual life of an *élite* of mankind. This union, however, was still not complete ; it did not extend to the animal-bodily life.

The Word was not fully made flesh till he came down from heaven and was conceived by the Virgin ; and this, too, was the act of the Spirit as well. In the Annunciation both the Word and the Spirit are sent to reveal Sophia to the world from the Father ; and thus to reveal, in the

earthly, the heavenly manhood.   The next point
to note in this mystery is that the Spirit must come
on the Virgin, and be accepted by her, before she
can conceive and give flesh to the Word.   Her
divine Infant is only conceived in the power of the
Spirit : it is not that the Spirit is given to crown
his conception.   In the Incarnation the Son and
the Spirit come down from heaven together ; for
the Spirit who rests on the Son inseparably and
unconfusedly, in his descent on the Virgin brings
down the Word too in person ; in virtue of which
she, conceiving the Son, becomes the Birthgiver
of God.

The Holy Spirit who thus eternally rests on the
Son and is therefore inseparable from his divinity,
while by " grace " (Luke ii. 40) he rests also upon
his humanity, at the Saviour's baptism further
descends on the latter in person.   And thereby
our Saviour becomes in the full sense the Christ,
and receives the anointing of the Holy Spirit,
who thus remains with him during the whole of
his ministry.   And here let us repeat once again
it is as the incarnate Word thus anointed with the
Holy Spirit that Christ, in Sophia the twofold
revelation of both divine persons, appears as the
Power and Wisdom of God (1 Cor. i. 24).   The
withdrawal of Christ from the world, in consequence of his ascension and sitting upon the right

hand of the Father, is from the first associated with the sending of that other Comforter whom in the last discourse he promised to send ; there follows the actual descent of the Spirit at Pente-cost. The full force of this fact too can only be seen in the light of the doctrine of God-manhood or of Sophia.

First of all we must grasp the relation between the persons of God involved in this mission. The originating hypostasis throughout remains, as before in all missions *ad extra*, the Father. Yet in fulfilling their mission, the other two persons completely change places. When the Word became flesh, the Spirit accomplished the will of the Father to send him, and, so far, himself seemed to send him. By contrast, at Pentecost, it is the Son who, it seems, sends the Spirit when he promises to " pray the Father " concerning this Comforter, that, in the name of the Son, the Father would send him (Jn. xv. 16 and 26). The fact that the days of his flesh are accomplished completes the circle and opens a new possibility for the descent of the Holy Spirit into the world, through the mediation of the Son.

Though the Word and the Life, the Son and the Spirit, are two, yet the bond which unites them appears in the one self-revelation they share in Sophia, alike in eternal God-manhood in God

and in the appearing in time among men of the
God-man. The other Comforter is sent into the
world not to bring it some new revelation, his
own, but to bring to completion that made by
the Son ; the content revealed is precisely the
same for them both. And this is expressed with
great force in our Saviour's promise to send him :
the two " Comforters " are distinct persons, inseparable as unconfused ; the comfort they bring
is the same. The Comforter when he descends
brings to the world life in Christ, proclaims Christ,
is the " Spirit of Christ " (1 Pet. i. 11) of whom it
can be said : " Now if any man have not the
spirit of Christ, he is none of his " (Rom. viii. 9);
" That the God of our Lord Jesus Christ, the
Father of glory, may give unto you the Spirit of
wisdom and revelation in the knowledge of him "
(Eph. i. 17) ; " The Spirit of Jesus " (Phil. i. 19 ;
with which compare Gal. iv. 6, and 1 Pet. i. 10–
12). Christ says of the Comforter, " He shall
teach you all things, and bring all things to your
remembrance, whatsoever I have said unto you"
(Jn. xiv. 26) ; " He shall testify of me " (xv. 26).
And, finally, a text which sums up all this reads
as follows : " Howbeit, when he the spirit of
truth is come, he will guide you into all truth :
For he shall not speak of himself ; but whatsoever
he shall hear, that shall he speak, and he will show

you things to come. . . . All things that the
Father hath are mine : therefore said I that he
shall take of mine, and shall show it unto you "
(xvi. 13 and 15). In such of the Fathers as the
great Athanasius, and Basil, we find the same
thought expressed thus : the Son is the image of
the Father, the Spirit is that of the Son. A
further fact, too, supports this. When Pentecost
came, and even immediately afterwards, the sole
and entire theme of the apostles' preaching was
neither the Holy Spirit nor the fact of Pentecost,
but the suffering and glory of Christ (cf. the first
sermon of Peter, Acts ii. 22–36).

Inevitably the question arises—what sense can
we put upon such references to the Holy Spirit,
which seem to attribute to him such an entirely
subservient and secondary place, compared with
the incarnate Word ? The Holy Spirit appears
to have no more to do than to spread the good
news of the God-man, and minister to him. As
to this we need only point out that it answers at all
points to that converse relation, which held at
our Lord's Incarnation : which the Holy Spirit
prepared and announced and led up to. Then
there is no question of " subordination ". In
giving flesh to the Word, the rôle ascribed to the
Spirit certainly does not belittle him. The
mutual relation between the Son and Spirit in

the Incarnation is evidence only of the double part played therein by Sophia, as heavenly and creaturely manhood at once. The whole revelation is one : the personal Word brought to fruit by the Holy Spirit ; and therefore this same Word is preached by the apostles, when moved by the Spirit. Yet this sort of transparency, in virtue of which it is the Word, not himself, which the Spirit reveals in himself, in God-manhood, is thoroughly consonant with that particular aspect of love in the Godhead which distinguishes God, the third Person. Life in the Spirit is then life in Christ, the inspiration of the Spirit gives knowledge of Christ, he who has not the Spirit of Christ is " none of his ". So closely are the two persons identified in this one revelation they share.

What was it that happened at Pentecost? What sort of barrier divides the whole life of the world up to, and after, that moment? From the beginning the spirit of God was at work in the world and his gifts were bestowed, in particular, under the old Covenant, and, still more, in the Incarnation of Christ. The new thing which happened at Pentecost was that there then entered the world not the " Spirit of God " in his gifts, but God the Spirit in person. Nor was the Spirit then given by measure, or bestowed on the Lord or his Mother alone, but also upon the apostles and all who were with them, and later upon the whole Church and the whole of the world. In the Holy Spirit Christ now sent to the world from the Father that other Comforter whom he had promised to send. To grasp the full force of this happening both in itself and in its connection with the Incarnation requires some effort. The wealth of its import can be compared with nought less.

As then it was the second Person of the Trinity which came down from heaven and took flesh, so here the third Person comes down to abide in the world. This coming from heaven is, on the one hand, in substance the same in each case ; on the other, the mode of its doing in each case is different. The difference is plain : while the Word is incarnate, the God-man revealed in person ; the Spirit is neither. Instead, he permeates humanity, abides with it, makes it divine. But the realization of God-manhood, by such a union between the divine and the human that creaturely manhood may share in the life of the heavenly God-manhood, is the end of both missions alike. In other words, each is a union, and even identification, of Sophia divine and created, which yet maintains the distinction between their two natures. In the Incarnation created Sophia, earthly manhood, receives, in the

Logos, the personal Wisdom of God. At the descent of the Spirit the same human nature receives the personal Spirit of Wisdom. The fullness of God-manhood can be achieved only through both events in conjunction, just as divine Sophia itself stands for revelation effected in the persons of either disclosing hypostasis, not in that of the Son or the Spirit alone, but in both in conjunction. If God-manhood had to depend on the Incarnation alone for its realization it must remain uncompleted. The same would be true if the gifts of the Spirit alone were in question, as in the Old Testament, or even the personal descent of the Spirit alone to the world. This latter in any case would be impossible had not the Incarnation preceded it. It is the Son who sends to the world from the Father the Spirit, the fruit of his own Incarnation. Here we are faced with the real connection between these two acts—the Incarnation and Pentecost ; and it is plain it reflects the relation between the two persons as such, in the Trinity, and in Sophia. Inseparably and unconfusedly united, both persons reveal the Father alike in eternal Wisdom and in creation, which is called into being by the Father, through the medium and participation of both. Hence the salvation and deification of that creation in God-manhood can be accomplished

only through both in conjunction. More than
this, the personal mission of either was only
effected by the aid of the other. This we have
already observed in regard to the Word taking
flesh, who was sent by the Father, and given flesh
by the Spirit. But Pentecost shows the same
feature, when through the Son the Spirit is sent
by the Father, so that the Spirit would seem to
be sent as the direct result of the prayer of the
Son to the Father. Here the Son and the Spirit,
it seems, exactly reverse their previous relation.

Why is this so ? It is because the historic
descent of the Holy Spirit into the world at large
only became possible as a consequence of the
Incarnation. As a result, when the Holy Spirit
comes into the world, it is as if he were coming
upon Christ incarnate once more. In the Holy
Trinity he eternally rests on the Son ; on Christ
the Incarnate Word he rests in his ministry and
subsequent glorification at the right hand of the
Father—for the Holy Spirit, whose hypostatic
love unites Father and Son, himself is this *dextera
Patris*, the heavenly glory bestowed on the God-
man. But the Son who, at his ascension to
heaven, appears to abandon the world and mankind, does not then in fact become dis-carnate,
nor does he relinquish his manhood or cut himself
off from the rest of creation. For the time being

his personal manhood, no less than his risen body, has been removed from the world, yet in the world there remains the manhood which belongs to him as the second Adam, already bound to him for ever, and likewise bound up with the world. This new mankind belongs to Christ and is pre-destined with him to be deified. Nevertheless, it is left orphaned when first the Ascension has taken away the Lord from it.

This link with Christ, this life in him, this pre-sent reality of his God-manhood in the world and its destined fulfilment, provide the field for the activity of the Holy Spirit upon his descent into the world. It is for this that the Holy Spirit is sent by the Son from the Father ; to bring to completion the work of Christ, to manifest him to the world, and to glorify the creature, even as the Father glorified the Son, by thus sending him. It is precisely as glory that he is sent to the world. That the third person of the Trinity at Pentecost descends into the world, not merely in the gifts then bestowed, but in person, is evident alike from the direct promise of our Lord in his last discourse and from many other passages of Scrip-ture (1 Cor. xii. 11 ; ii. 10–11 ; Rom. viii. 26–27 ; Eph. iv. 30 ; Acts xiii. 2). It is true that the Spirit's hypostasis in this, unlike that of the Son, remains hidden from us. In the present age the

Holy Spirit is revealed to us only in his gifts, in
" grace ". As regards the personal descent of
the Holy Spirit the significance of Pentecost remains a mystery to us, though Pentecost is, as
it were, now prolonged in the history of the
Church, and in the hidden depths of the Church
the process is already completed ; the Holy
Spirit in person has entered the world and abides
in it.

But the actual manner of his descent and abiding differs from that of the Incarnation. The
" descent from heaven " of the Son is accompanied by his kenosis. He voluntarily forsakes
his glory, divests himself of his divine preroga-
tives. He seems, in fact, to leave heaven :
though this by no means implies any cessation or
interruption of the life of the Deity in the Logos
himself. This process is reversed later on by his
return to heaven at the Ascension. The descent
of the Holy Spirit involves no such kenosis. He
in his descent from heaven does not forsake it—
he does not lessen his divinity and his glory. For
indeed the Holy Spirit is himself the glory of the
Godhead. The Holy Spirit coming down, without leaving heaven, from on high, completes the
link between God and creation, initiated in the
Incarnation. Yet, as the Incarnation required
the *personal* descent of the Son, so here the action

or gifts of the Spirit alone would not be enough. His *personal* coming was needed. This inner connection between the work of the Incarnation and the bestowal of the gifts of the Spirit is vigorously emphasized in the last discourse of our Lord.

We are faced with the fundamental fact that two hypostases, and not one, are sent from on high to the world. God-manhood in process of being accomplished presupposes the union of the divine and human natures, or of divine and created Wisdom, in the one hypostasis of the Logos. But this union has to be effected by the Holy Spirit, more than that, *is* Holy Spirit. And this bond will be ultimately realized and sealed in the life of Christ in man and man in Christ. The consummation of this union, which is, as it were, a new manifestation or renewal of Christ's Incarnation, is the descent of the Holy Spirit. Descending from heaven, it is as though he brought the incarnate Christ afresh in the capacity of " another Comforter " (Jn. xiv. 16–18). This points to the mystery of Christ's abiding in the world in the Holy Spirit ; never is Christ separated from the Holy Spirit. So God-manhood, like the Incarnation itself, is the work not of one person, but two—the Son and the Spirit together. This principle of duality holds good alike for the divine and the creaturely Sophia or

God-manhood, and for the manifestation of God in the world. Christ and the Holy Spirit together are the one Comfort, although the Comforter is two in one ; one God-manhood, accomplished in two hypostases.

The Holy Spirit descends into the world once for all, never to return or be withdrawn from it. On the contrary, we see that he makes ready for the second coming of Christ into the world, as God-manhood manifest. This coming will bring with it that hypostatic revelation of the Holy Spirit, which is not given to us in this present age, in so far as the abiding presence of the Holy Spirit in the world manifests itself only as yet in his gifts. These gifts are many and various. What they are appears, though by no means exhaustively, in the Acts as well as the Epistles. All there appear as divine inspiration of man, a union between inspired human endeavour and divine inspiration, bestowed in response to it. It is accomplished, as it were, in the coincidence of two principles, *ex opere operantis* and *ex opere operato*. But the action of the Holy Spirit is by no means restricted to the realm of the spirit, it extends to the whole world of physical nature, sanctifying and transfiguring it from within. So, too, the Parousia, the second coming of Christ, is accomplished by a transfiguration of the world,

by the vision of a new heaven and a new earth, by
the descent of the Heavenly Jerusalem.   And all
this is the work of the Holy Spirit, who manifests
the power of our Lord's Incarnation, and acts as
the Spirit of Christ.

The distinctive and characteristic feature of the
action of the Holy Spirit in the world and in man
may be said to be his *adaptability* to the creature's
capacity to receive him.   The Holy Spirit gives
himself " by measure " and " measure for measure ".   It is only in relation to the Son of God,
by contrast with all creation, that it is said :
" God giveth not the Spirit by measure *unto him* "
(Jn. iii. 34).   This measure is such as not to burn
up the creature, or destroy its corruptible nature,
but to make it possible for it to bear him.   It is
for this reason that the Holy Spirit restricts the
full force of his action.   In a similar manner he
attunes and adapts his will to that of the creature,
in analogy with the way in which the two natures
in the God-man, with their two wills and two
energies, were co-ordinated, to make the lower
accord with the higher.

But in Christ this concord was established
within the realm of his person.   While the Holy
Spirit, without becoming incarnate in separate
persons, himself permeating them all, extends to
each individual the call : " Behold, I stand at the

door and knock " (Rev. iii. 20). Grace accords
with human freedom, it never violates this freedom ; it educates and prepares it. But this
voluntary self-restriction, out of love for the
creature and respect for its creaturely freedom,
constitutes the *kenosis* of the third hypostasis,
which is peculiar to it by virtue of its proper part
in God-manhood. It is beyond human comprehension or reason *how* the almighty and all-holy
God can restrict himself in his action. Man will
never be given to understand how the Absolute
could restrict himself in the creation of the world.
But this kenosis of the Spirit, as an aspect of
sacrificial love, of necessity springs from the
special form of divine ministration in which " all
is given by the Holy Spirit "[1], yet only when
human freedom is willing to acquiesce and accept.

The *kenosis* of the third Person thus differs from
that of the second, which in the Incarnation
forsakes, as it were, its divinity, and adjusts
even its proper activity to the highest measure
of human nature, seen in its purity and holiness
in the God-man. While the Holy Spirit does
not abandon his divinity and is not united with
human nature, but penetrates it. But when
he penetrates it he always measures his action
in accordance with the weakness of the creature.

[1] From the stichera for the feast of Pentecost ; cf. the *Veni Creator*.

The kenosis of the Son extends only to the period of his earthly ministry, and ends with his glorification. The kenosis of the Holy Spirit, strictly speaking, began with the very creation when the Holy Spirit charged himself to preserve and to quicken the creature according to its own capacity. But the fullness of his kenosis only takes place at his coming at Pentecost and lasts till the fullness of God-manhood shall be attained, when God shall be all in all. Consequently, this epoch of kenosis extends at any rate over the whole of this present age of the " Church militant ", of the kingdom of grace, which is ultimately to be succeeded by the kingdom of glory. Christ's enthronement on earth, and his kingly ministry, is accomplished and extended in the world by the power of the Holy Spirit, in whom " the Kingdom of God is come in power ". This then is Pentecost ; the fruit of the Incarnation, the penetration of the creature by Wisdom, the union of the divine and created Sophia in the power of the Spirit—God-manhood.

All that has been said above undoubtedly leads to an *eschatological* concept of Pentecost. Its full significance will only be clear in the Parousia of Christ and the transfiguration of the world. There will be no special Parousia of the Holy Spirit, for he comes into the world to remain in it ; but there will be, as it were, a new manifestation of Pentecost in all its power and, most important of all, in the *personal* revelation of the third hypo- stasis, that which at present we lack. We perceive the life of the Spirit by the grace of the Spirit and we know holiness by his holiness, but we do not know the Holy Spirit himself, we do not know his personal likeness.[1] That will become known to mankind only in the Parousia of the Son which in this sense will be also a parousia of the Holy Spirit, the full revelation of divine Sophia in its dual aspect, and of the two hypostases which dis- close the Father. It follows necessarily from this that the third hypostasis will take a special part in the resurrection, in the last judgment and in the glorification of creation. For the " kingdom prepared from the foundation of the world " (Matt. xxv. 34) is precisely the Holy Spirit. In the most ancient version of the text of the Lord's Prayer we read—" may the Holy Spirit come " instead of " Thy kingdom come ". For this reason when the significance of Pentecost is ex- pounded in S. Peter's discourse, immediately after the event, he makes use of a passage from Joel which is definitely eschatological (Acts ii. 16–21 : Joel ii. 28–32). The promise that " God may be all in all " (1 Cor. xv. 28) refers to the full mani-

[1] *See* Ch. VI below.

festation of the divine in the creaturely Sophia, to that deification of the creature, which is to be accomplished by the power of Christ in the Holy Spirit.

THE VENERATION OF OUR LADY

CHAPTER VI

THE VENERATION OF OUR LADY

THE Church venerates the Mother of God as
" more honourable than the cherubim, more
glorious incomparably than the seraphim ", as
the " heavenly Queen ", whom " all the elements,
heaven and earth, air and sea obey ". In number-
less prayers and hymns her glory and grandeurs
are extolled.

The Protestant mind, by some curious insensi-
bility, quite fails to appreciate the position which
belongs to the Virgin Mary, not only in the incarnation, but in the whole life of the Church.
Our veneration of the Mother of God seems to it
to border on idolatry. In this connection it is
apposite to refer to the fact of her full *deification*,
in virtue of which she is manifested as the heart
and glory of the world. For us, the dogma of the
divine maternity of our Lady is fully illumined
only in the light of the doctrine of Sophia, the
divine Wisdom in creation.

Orthodoxy does not share the latest catholic
dogma, the 1854 definition of the Immaculate

173

Conception, in so far as her exemption from original sin in virtue of this " immaculate conception " distinguishes the Mother of God from the rest of mankind and seems consequently to render her incapable of imparting to her divine son the authentic manhood of the old Adam, with its need of redemption. The blessed Virgin, since she is truly human, shares with humanity both its original sin and also that inherent infirmity of human nature, which finds its extreme expression in an inevitable, natural death.

However, the force of original sin, which varies generally from man to man, is in her reduced to the point of a mere possibility, never to be actualized. In other words, the blessed Virgin knows no *personal* sin ; she was manifestly sanctified by the Holy Ghost from the very moment of her conception. In numerous liturgical texts, such as those which refer to her Conception, Nativity or Presentation, she is called " the spiritual heaven ", " holiest of the holy ", " divine and most pure temple of the spirit ", " pure from her infancy ", and so forth. More than that, she is spoken of as " mother elect before all ages, made known as mother of God unto succeeding years ", " beloved by God from all eternity ". With this accords also her final glorification when her son honoured her death by her resurrection and

assumption into heaven ; a doctrine contained in
the office for the feast of the Dormition.

Of course, this glory is bestowed upon the
blessed Virgin only in view of her part in the
Incarnation. Consequently, we can distinguish
a twofold act : it is the descent of the Word from
heaven to become man and assume his human
nature, which is announced by the lips of the
blessed Mother of God : " behold the handmaid
of the Lord, be it unto me according to thy word "
(Lk. i. 38). But for that to be possible, there
must already have appeared upon earth a human
being who should be worthy of the archangel's
mission in the Annunciation and capable of response to it. The whole force of righteousness,
accumulated in the Old Testament church, and
by a line of saints (the " genealogy "), was here
united with her personal exceeding holiness and
humility of heart.

Mary was manifestly apt for the Holy Ghost to
descend upon her. But he eternally abides upon
the Son. Therefore, in receiving the Spirit she,
at the same time, conceived the Son, who is inseparable from him, and became Mother of God.
Her humanity became his humanity.[1] In Christ

[1] In the prayer of S. Simeon the Meditative, in preparation for
Holy Communion, we read : " Thou didst take upon thyself by the
infusion of the Holy Ghost and at the good pleasure of the everlasting Father, together with the pure and virginal blood of her
who bare thee, our whole compound nature."

this human nature was united with the divine nature, received the divine personality of the Word, and was taken up into God-manhood. In Mary this same human nature which she gave to Christ remained in its original human condition, with the personality of the Virgin, though now sanctified by the Holy Ghost and becoming spirit-bearing. The birth of Christ from the Virgin is not merely an isolated event in time ; it establishes an eternally abiding bond between Mother and Son ; so that an image of our Lady which depicts her with her infant in her arms is in fact an image of God-manhood.

The fact that our Lady is spirit-bearing did not make her theandric nor constitute an incarnation of the Holy Ghost. For the Holy Ghost is not the subject but the principle, of the Incarnation. He abides, however, in the ever-virgin Mary as in a holy temple, while her human personality seems to become transparent to him and to provide him with a human countenance. We must distinguish the different stages in this overshadowing of the virgin by the Holy Ghost.

First of all, in this connection, comes her peculiar and exclusive sanctification by the grace of the Holy Ghost, shown in her conception, nativity and presentation in the temple, and throughout her holy childhood and maidenhood. Next

follows the personal descent of the Holy Ghost at
the Annunciation which consecrated her whole
bodily being and made of her the Mother of
God.

The consecration of the temple of her body
could not, of course, be accomplished without a
further sanctification also of her soul. The end
was not yet, however : she had soon, in company
with her son, and treading in his footsteps, to
travel the road of his earthly ministry, to receive
the " sword in her heart " all the way to her
station by the cross on Golgotha, where she had to
suffer a spiritual death with him upon the cross,
in order, with him, to enter into his glory. This
entry into the glory of her son was completed for
his most pure mother at Pentecost. Then, together with the apostles, but of course in superabundant fullness, she received the outpouring of
the Holy Spirit. And this in turn prepared her
for the prolongation and consummation of her
glory at her falling asleep. For her it was a
second Pentecost—she had had her first at the
Annunciation. Now she became wholly possessed
by the Spirit, and received from Christ that glory
which he had from the Father, for those to " behold ", as he said, " whom thou hast given me "
(John xvii. 34), and first of all his Mother. It is
in the setting of this process of glorification that

we must understand also the resurrection and assumption into heaven of the Mother of God. Both alike are essentially *anticipations* of what is prepared for the humanity of the whole Christ in the risen life ; both were bestowed in advance upon the Mother of God at her Assumption. Although following the law of human nature, she tasted natural death, yet " death could not detain her ", for her humanity is at the same time that of Christ himself, who is the well of life.

As he is risen, so she, too, has her resurrection, though of course, otherwise than he who is the God-man. She was raised by him in the same way as, at his second coming, he is to raise all mankind. This resurrection of his mother Christ, of course, accomplishes, like the future general resurrection, in the power of the Holy Spirit, " the giver of life ". For her, it manifests her peculiar dignity of spirit-bearer.[1] But the very fact that her resurrection takes place *before* that of the rest of mankind already sets her above this world and is in this sense her assumption into heaven, sometimes more narrowly defined in liturgical texts as her session " at the right hand of her Son ".

[1] This thought finds expression in a symbol characteristic of the Western church, though not unknown also in the East, that of the glorification of the most holy Mother of God (or her Coronation), in so far as glorification is a work of the Trinity " appropriated " to the Holy Ghost.

Evidently, it is necessary to avoid a dogmatic identification of the Assumption and the Ascension. Indeed, they must be distinguished, and even, in rigour, contrasted. Christ's Ascension and return to the bosom of the Holy Trinity we find connected with his descent from heaven to be made man. It betokens the end of the kenosis of God the Son. The Assumption of the Mother of God on the other hand, is a notable, even an extreme, instance of the glorification of a creature, deified and sharing in the life of God, by participation. It by no means denotes a penetration into the Holy Trinity, which is metaphysically beyond the reach of any creature. It means no more than incorporation into the life of the Godhead : that life in Christ and through the Spirit of Christ, wherein " God shall be all in all ". It is precisely this—no more, but also no less—which is denoted by the figure of her session " at the right hand " of her Son.

Indeed, the Assumption of the Mother of God does not even denote any estrangement or metaphysical removal from the world, which is in fact impossible, being at variance with the law of created nature. The Church frankly testifies that the Mother of God " at her falling asleep did not forsake the world " (Troparion, Aug. 15). In spite of her assumption she will continue to belong to the world, although established in glory *above* the world ; on a level, so to speak, midway between creation and the heaven of God. Her beneficent presence in, and peculiar nearness to, the world is manifested not only by the common mind of the Church at prayer, but also in her repeated appearances, in miraculous images, visions granted to the saints, and so forth.

In the resurrection and assumption of our Lady the creation of the world may be said to be completed, and its end achieved : " wisdom is justified of her children " (Mt. xi. 19). In her the world has already become glorious, divine and worthy of the regard of God. The Mother of God, since she gave to her son the manhood of the second Adam, is also the mother of the race of man, of universal humanity, the spiritual centre of the whole creation, the heart of the world. In her, creation is utterly and completely divinized, conceives, bears and fosters God.

In relation to the Father she is named Daughter, in relation to the Word, Mother and Bride, unwedded Bride of God, while in relation to the Holy Ghost she is the Spirit-bearer, the glory of the world. In this sense she is the heart of the Church, its centre and its personal embodiment. In relation to the Saints, she is united with them in the Church in glory, and presents her petitions

for the world, for which we unceasingly solicit her.
Yet in her intercourse with heaven, sitting at the
right hand of her Son, she stands higher than all
the saints, and takes precedence even of the world
of angels, in view of her part in the mystery of the
Incarnation.

It is in this sense alone that the Church makes
use of the prayer : " Holy Mother of God, save
us ".[1] She has been given power, as Queen of
heaven, by virtue of that power over heaven and
earth which was granted to her son. Evidently
the two are not identical : for the power of Christ
is that which belongs to the divine person of the
God-man ; while to his Mother power is given
corresponding to her complete deification and
participation in the glory of her son.

Moreover she is the appointed intercessor for
the human race, blessing them with her protecting veil in a peculiar sense, otherwise than do the
saints in general by their prayers and intercessions.
For the saints have still to grow in holiness, going
from strength to strength along the way of progressive sanctification. And besides, they still
remain on the *hither side* of the resurrection region,

---

[1] This usage by no means connotes that our Lady is either an
associate or a subaltern Saviour of the world. It must be understood only in conjunction with other references to her, asking the
aid of her prayers. It connotes merely the singular power of her
prayerful intercession—no more.

to reach which they await the second coming of Christ, while our Lady's resurrection is already accomplished. That is yet to come for them, which for her has already come to pass. She has arrived at that *fullness* of the godlike life of grace which for the rest of creation remains to be revealed. Therefore the Mother of God remains *inaccessible* to the world, for she is above the world, and if she appears to it, that is only in virtue of her loving condescension, a kind of self-abasement proper to her.

Jacob's ladder, set up between heaven and earth, was a figure of our Lady. The complete manifestation of the mother of God to the world will only be possible when the world itself enters into the kingdom of glory in virtue of the general resurrection and all creation is transfigured. So iconography depicts the holy Mother in the last judgment at the right hand of her son, where she appears to intercede with him for a world of sinners ; and, indeed, according to the belief of the Church, she does assist souls along the path which she herself travelled at her falling asleep.

The veneration of our Lady in Orthodoxy is such that those outside may well ask the question : Is not this frankly exaggerated ? Does it not introduce into Christian doctrine the figure of a goddess ? Such a misapprehension may be dissipated by the simple consideration that our Lady, however exalted may be the honour paid her, is not divine, is not even theandric. Her human nature and personality subsist in spite of her complete deification. Though she, upon whom the Holy Ghost reposes, is therefore spirit-bearing, yet for all that she remains a woman, however fully deified. The Holy Ghost is not personally incarnate like the Son. In conformity with his personal nature he blesses, sanctifies, penetrates and vivifies, and that is all. And yet his fullest and loftiest manifestation is nevertheless effected in the spirit-bearing " blessed " virgin Mary. She is, in personal form, the human likeness of the Holy Ghost. Through her, with her human form become entirely transparent to the Holy Ghost, we have a manifestation and, as it were, a personal revelation of him.

The person of the Holy Ghost remains hidden from us even in his descent at Pentecost, which conferred immediately only the *gifts* of the Spirit.[1] But there is a human person to whom it is given to manifest the Holy Ghost himself, and that is the most holy virgin, Mary, the heart of the Church. And yet this *manifestation* of the Holy Ghost—let us emphasize the fact that it is precisely a manifestation, not an incarnation—

[1] For Pentecost, *see* my work *The Paraclete*.

remains for us in this life beyond our understanding.

It vanished from the world with the event of the death, resurrection and Assumption of our Lady ; her glorified likeness is unknown to the world, which cannot yet receive its revelation of the Holy Ghost. It concerns only the age to come, and will belong to the last things. Together with the appearance of the glorified Christ at his coming again in glory the world will behold his glorified humanity in the person of the spirit-bearer, the virgin Mary.

God-manhood is to be found " on earth as it is in heaven "—in a double, not only a single, form : not only that of the God-man, Christ, but that of his mother too. Jesus-Mary—there is the fullness of God-manhood. The internal self-disclosure of the Holy Trinity is marked by this same duality : the revelation of the Father is made through the Son and Spirit together, inseparably and unconfusedly. In like manner, in the Incarnation, the Son is " conceived by the Holy Ghost, born of the virgin Mary ". She is the personal subject of the humanity of Christ, and his feminine counterpart. The image of the mother of God with her child is an expression of this Incarnation or God-manhood. To separate Christ from his mother (still more to forget her, as historical

Protestantism has done) is in effect an attempted violation of the mystery of the Incarnation, in its innermost shrine.

Yet the veneration of the Virgin extends not merely to her divine maternity, but also to herself. Accordingly she is depicted in certain of her icons apart from the Holy Child, as the " Unwedded Bride ", as " Ever-Virgin ".[1] This conception of her perpetual Virginity is as it were a personification of the Church, the glorified creation, the Bride of the Lamb ; and it is in this sense that the expressions of the " Song of Songs " concerning the mystical marriage of Christ and the Church are most often understood, alike in East and West. Rightly, then, does this figure of " created Wisdom " hold its central position in the shrine of Sophia, the Wisdom of God, at Kiev. And with this we reach the sophiological aspect of the doctrine and cultus of our Lady.

Without entering into a detailed discussion of the origin and significance of the change, it does seem to be an admitted fact of history, of considerable dogmatic interest, that the shrines of Sophia, the Wisdom of God, which for Byzantium

---

[1] For example, the mosaic in the sanctuary apse of the ancient cathedral of St. Sophia at Kiev, known as " the Impregnable Wall ", or the icon of " the Compassion ", before which St. Seraphim of Sarov used to pray, excellently reproduced in A. F. Dobbie-Bateman *St. Seraphim of Sarov*, London 1936, and elsewhere.

bore a Christological meaning, received a Mario-logical interpretation in Russia. They were dedicated under the title of our Lady, and their feasts of title, in accordance with Russian usage, came to be celebrated on her feasts[1]—at Kiev on the day of her Nativity, at Novgorod and elsewhere on that of her Dormition. Thus the cult of the Wisdom of God received a Marial character.

The Christ-Sophia of Byzantium was completed in Russia by a Marial Sophia. This development found expression alike in iconography and in liturgy. Either the icons of Sophia are given a frankly Marial theme[2] or they display a complex dogmatic composition in which our Lady is still assigned her place.[3] A rich field of material for this purpose is supplied by the offices of her feasts, such as her Nativity and Presentation in the Temple, wherein is disclosed her predestination from eternity,[4] her " pre-election " in the ways

[1] It is natural to reckon as a Mario-Sophianic feast that of the Intercession of the Virgin, celebrated particularly in Russia : it refers to the protection which she extends to the world.

[2] Here we must note the church icon in the Cathedral of St. Sophia at Kiev—evidently of western origin—of the Mother of God as Wisdom (following Wisdom ix, 1 and ff.) and as the Church.

[3] In this connection the chief significance belongs to the Novgorod compositions for an icon of Wisdom, as a fiery angel, with our Lady on the right side and St. John the Baptist on the left. *See* v. d. Mensbrugghe, *From Dyad to Triad*, London 1935.

[4] It is characteristic that for these feasts Proverbs ix is always included among the Old Testament lessons, while on the Annunciation there is added to this Proverbs viii, 22-35, which adds the Mario-Sophianic interpretation of Wisdom (in reference to Christ, on the contrary, this lesson is never employed).

of Providence, which in a true sense may be set on a parallel with that of the Lamb " foreordained before the foundation of the world " (1 Pet. i. 20). There even exists a proper office of Sophia, the Wisdom of God, which is combined with the office of the Dormition. Its fundamental pecu- liarity is this, that the several texts of its prayers and hymns lend a twofold significance to Sophia. The Christo-Sophianic and the Mario-Sophianic interpretation are there simultaneously present. Sophia is equated at once with Christ and with the Mother of God. This duality points to the peculiar sophiological conception which we have now to unfold with regard to the Mother of God.

It is possible to find a double source of this identification of our Lady with Sophia, the Wisdom of God and to give it, accordingly, a two- fold interpretation. In the first place our Lady can be given the name of Sophia, in so far as she is the Spirit-bearer, in virtue of the personal descent upon her of the Holy Ghost ; she is his consecrated temple. Although she does not thereby become theandric, since the Holy Ghost is not incarnate, yet she is his anointed vessel. Wisdom in the Godhead is both the Son and the Holy Ghost. If the Logos is Wisdom, so too is the Holy Ghost, since he is the Spirit of Wisdom. And the cultus of our Lady as Wisdom may refer to her *position* of Spirit-bearer, personally over-shadowed by the Holy Ghost, therefore not to her personally, but through her to the Holy Ghost himself. And in that sense it is to be taken as veneration of the *divine* Wisdom.

But besides this we find another meaning attached to the veneration of our Lady, in so far as it is directed to *created* Wisdom. She *is* created Wisdom, for she is creation glorified. In her is realized the purpose of creation, the complete penetration of the creature by wisdom, the full accord of the created type with its Prototype, its entire accomplishment. In her creation is completely irradiated by its prototype. In her God is already all in all. The limits to the pene-tration of creation by wisdom, involved in its freedom to develop, are entirely transcended in the "handmaid of the Lord", who is already worthy of the glory of heaven. Divine Wisdom shines forth in creaturely form in the complete holiness of her who is "more honourable than the cherubim, more glorious incomparably than the seraphim". For ontological holiness is at the same time fully realized wisdom, wherein "wisdom is justified of her children" (Mt. xi. 19). In this aspect of Wisdom manifest in our Lady it is precisely her *creatureliness* which appears to be essential, her created human nature, which was found worthy to be honoured with the bestowal of the Holy Ghost.

It is impossible, however, to exclude the Christological aspect of this line of thought. The Mother of God is glorified with the title of Wisdom only in so far as she is Mother of the God-man, who took from her his human nature, the counterpart of created Wisdom. According to the sophiological interpretation of the definition of Chalcedon, the two natures in Christ correspond to the two forms of Sophia, the divine and the created. The created humanity of Christ the God-man came to him from the Mother of God. It belongs to her. In a true sense it is possible to say that she herself personally is this created manhood of Christ, that she is the created Sophia. The manhood of Christ belongs at once to him, since it is one of his two natures, and to her, in whom it personally subsists. And it is in this sense, as sharing the human nature of the God-man, that his holy Mother is the created Sophia. In this way the different aspects of Sophia, the Wisdom of God, its two faces, are at one in the person of the Mother of God. And this fact is reflected in the complexity of the dogmatic expression of her relationship to the Wisdom of God.

Thus it is that the most holy Mother of God is the created Sophia, and is acknowledged and venerated as such by the piety of the Church of Russia. Therefore is she exalted as " more honourable than the cherubim, more glorious incomparably than the seraphim " and, *a fortiori*, holiest of the human race. Yet even the holy Mother of God is not the only manifestation of created Wisdom.[1] Ontologically it includes, in it is grounded the existence of the whole creation, " heaven and earth ", the world of angels and the world of men. Consequently their mutual relation is that which holds between exemplar and substantial forms, as in the Platonic world of ideas and its realization in empirical fact, in becoming. Yet it is not enough to establish merely this ontological connection between creation and its source in Wisdom, for such a connection holds also for the fallen creation, even for the devil and all whom he has seduced, both angels and men.

Created Wisdom serves not only as the foundation of creation, but also as the means of its glorification, its potential glory. The penetration by Wisdom of the creation, which itself rests upon the basis of Wisdom, is its proper work, in the form which particularly belongs to it, that of the *sanctity* of the creature. And in this again

---

[1] To the doctrine of created Wisdom is consecrated my dogmatic trilogy : 1. *The Burning Bush* (on our Lady) ; 2. *The Friend of the Bridegroom* (on St. John the Baptist) ; 3. *Jacob's Ladder* (on the Angels) Paris 1927, 1928, 1929, YMCA Press.

Wisdom is at one with the most holy Mother of
God, who is the summit of creation, the Queen of
heaven and earth.   From this point of view the
sanctity of the creature and its penetration by
wisdom is one and the same thing.   Yet it is still
necessary to draw a distinction.

To begin with, let us confine ourselves to the
world of angels.   After that probation which
witnessed the fall of Lucifer and his angels, those
angels who were confirmed in grace, with the
archangel Michael at their head (Rev. xii. 7–11)
entered upon the state of glory ; and since then,
bearing the marks of glory, they exemplify created
Wisdom in the world of bodiless spirits.   Why
then do even they, for all their nearness to the
throne of God—so terrifying to us—yet seem to
stand incomparably lower than the holy Mother
of God ?   We must see the reason of this, on the
one hand, in their present provisional relationship
towards the world of men, with which they are
united in a kind of fellow-manhood in virtue of
the ministry which they fulfil therein (the very
name " angels " signifies ministers of God to the
world of men).   The Fall separated the angels
from men.   The Incarnation united them anew
(Jn. i. 51) in the person of the God-man, but as
yet far from completely on the part of mankind.
For the rest, it still remains to undergo judgment

and pass that subsequent parting of the ways
before the state of glory, when angels themselves
are to be judged (1 Cor. vi. 3), apparently upon
the execution of their service. Therefore until
the glorification of man and the full manifestation
of his God-manhood, even the angels do not enjoy
the fullness of their glory, for they have yet part
of their course to run. Meanwhile, the holy
Mother of God has already attained the fullness of
her glory, she is in heaven, set above the angels,
who indeed worship her, as sharing with her Son
the manhood of the God-man.

She has not to come to judgment. But this
judgment awaits both men and angels, who
reach the term of their assimilation to man only
with the second coming of Christ (Mt. xxv. 31).
And, accordingly, what is said of the God-man
extends also, though indirectly, to the Mother
of God : " being made so much better than the
angels, as (he) hath by inheritance obtained a
more excellent name than they " (Heb. i. 4). It
is the *plenitude* of creation which is manifest in the
Mother of God, which makes her " incomparably " more excellent than the relatively unful-
filled world of bodiless spirits, appointed to render
angelic service to the world of men. Nevertheless,
in virtue of their holiness the holy angels, with
the archangel of the Annunciation at their head,

appear to form the immediate *entourage* of the holy Mother of God ; thus the liturgical chants extol her : " O thou who art full of grace, thou art the joy of every creature : the host of angels and the race of men "; thus, too, icons depict her. The angels *serve* the holy Mother of God, recognizing in her the full expression of created Wisdom. For them, too, she is their " Lady " and the heavenly " Queen ".

She is united by her holiness also with the *Saints,* in so far as they, in their own holiness, display the likeness of created Wisdom, bear the marks of Christ, are sealed with the Holy Ghost, and form part of God-manhood.   Indeed she has closer connections here than with the world of angels, for, being human, the Mother of God is Mother also of the whole human race, the centre of mankind.   But she stands contrasted to the rest of mankind and elevated above it, in so far as she abides already above or beyond the world in its present age, with death and resurrection now behind her.   In her is revealed all the fullness of the glory of the world ; now nothing can be added to it.   And at the last agony of the age, in the terrible judgment of Christ, she will be present only in order to intercede.   Even in the very greatest saints that inward discernment of good and evil must be accomplished, though

almost all emerge scatheless in the power of the
good.   In her there is no room for any such dis-
crimination : " thou art all fair, my love ; there is
no spot in thee " (Song of Songs iv. 7).

While, of course, all the saints are sanctified
by the Holy Ghost, and thereby incorporated
into the life of Christ, she is the Temple of the
Holy Ghost himself, wherein the Son of God
awaits his birth from her.   And nevertheless she
is encircled by those of " her own race ",[1] by
the saints of mankind, whose nearness to her is
measured by their sanctity.   Among them, at the
head of all humanity sanctified by Wisdom, stand
the two Johns, the Forerunner and the Divine ;
the latter in virtue of his position as her adopted
son, gained at the foot of the Cross, the former in
virtue of his nearness to Christ.   Only one stands
nearer to him than John the Baptist, and that one
is his Mother.   From Christ himself the Forerunner received the designation of greatest among
them that are born of women (Mt. xi. 11).   The
service he performed as Forerunner and Baptist,
" the friend of the Bridegroom ", meeting and
acknowledging Christ in the days of his flesh, sets
him above the apostles, indeed above all the elect
who have, in whatever degree, drawn near to

[1] " He is of our race " said our Lady of St. Seraphim, when she
appeared to him,

Christ. His ministry is designated as that of an
" angel " (Mal. iii. 1, cf. Mk. i. 2 ; Mt. xi. 10 ;
Lk. vii. 27), with a mysterious suggestion that he
is somehow peculiarly and personally connected
with the world of angels. His sanctification by
the Holy Ghost while yet in his mother's womb
(Lk. i. 44), the whole austere asceticism of his
figure, all that spiritual strength given him in
order to stand face to face with Christ, to accom-
plish the baptism of the God-man, to be a witness
of the mysterious theophany which accompanied
it and of the manifestation of Christ to the world,
all combine to oblige us to recognize his exceeding
personal holiness, even perhaps a personal
" exemption " from sin rendering him akin to
the Holy Virgin herself.

In this connection we should give heed to the
witness of the Church's imagery, which commonly
sets his likeness in immediate proximity to that of
Christ, nearer than any other saints and even the
angels, with the one exception of the Mother of
God. The blessed Virgin is depicted on the right
hand of Christ, John the Forerunner on his left.
We observe the same thing on the iconostasis
dividing the altar from the nave ; so too in the
icon known as the Deësis (δέησις—petition) and
in the composition of various other icons. It is
particularly to our purpose to note here again

the Novgorod icon of Sophia, depicted in the guise of a fiery angel, with the Mother of God standing on the right, and the Forerunner on the left. These two would seem here to depict created Wisdom in conjunction with the symbolic figure of heavenly Wisdom.

And yet with all this the distinction still holds good, which divides the mother of God from the rest of creation ; even the Forerunner remains as yet on *the hither side* of the resurrection. As regards his body he still belongs to this world and has to await his part in the general resurrection ; whereas our Lady was raised straightway upon her falling asleep. However, the Forerunner will be present at the last judgment, according to the evidence of the Church's imagery, in a position unlike that of the generality of those who are there to be judged. He will be present as a witness, or possibly, like the holy Mother of God, as an intercessor. For of him in particular was said, by the mouth of the Judge himself : " Wisdom is justified of her children " (Mt. xi. 19). In him, as in the Mother of God, the Wisdom of God is already manifest in creation.

CHAPTER VII

THE CHURCH

CHAPTER VII

THE CHURCH[1]

WHAT is the Church? This question has come to the forefront of Christian theological thought since the time of the Reformation and still to-day occupies unquestionably the first place therein. It is fair to say that it forms the chief difficulty in the path of the re-union movement, in its persistent endeavours to reassemble the outwardly divided fragments of the Church. Commonly, before defining the Church, theologians set out to debate and determine its various characteristics from what one may call its " phenomenology ", from the existence as a fact of the " visible " Church. Comparatively few stop to consider what we may call the " ontology " of the Church, that " invisible " foundation of its existence to which the baptismal creed refers in the phrase " I believe in . . ." the Church. Though it has, of course, its empirically visible

[1] *See* Bulgakov, *The Orthodox Church*; London, 1935. Also in *Puit* (The Way) in Russian, *An Outline of the Doctrine of the Church.*

199

embodiment, yet the Church itself is evidently outside the scope of our empirical mode of knowledge ; it is, in fact, matter of faith—" the evidence of things not seen " (Heb. xi. 1). The Church is more than an institution which happened to appear at a definite period in history, it is more than a congregation of men based on a true fellowship of spirit in doctrine and discipline ; it is, in fact, more than the whole of its history. More than that, the Church transcends history, and belongs primarily not to time alone, but to eternity. It is not merely that it is of divine institution, its very mode of existence is divine ; and its existence in God is prior to, antecedes, or more exactly, conditions its historical existence.

The Church is properly uncreated and yet it enters into the history of mankind. That implies that it has a theandric character ; it is, in fact, God-manhood *in actu*. According to the expression of the " Shepherd of Hermas " God created the world for the sake of the Church. That is as much as to say that it is at once the ground and goal of the world, its final cause and entelechy. The world of men by its creation is already designated to and for its deification, in the Incarnation and Pentecost. And this deification, which whether virtual or actual, is the supreme actualization of the world, is effected through the Church which thus appears as a ladder joining heaven and earth and conveying divine life to the creation. It follows from this that, in so far as it is grounded in God, the Church is divine Wisdom. And equally, in its earthly, historical existence, it is created Wisdom. In short, in the Church the two aspects of Wisdom mutually permeate one another and are entirely, inseparably and unconfusedly, united. The divine shines through the created Wisdom. The definition at Chalcedon of the mode of union of the two natures in Christ was at bottom a definition of the Church. The same would seem to apply to another dogma, as yet indeed unformulated, yet held as a fact by the Church—the descent of the Holy Ghost at Pentecost into the life of creation and the spirit of man. It is not possible to reach a final understanding or a correct expression of the doctrine of the Church save by starting from the fundamental theses of sophiology.

Consequently, in order to understand the Church, as a local community persisting through time and existing in different places, under the old and the new Covenants and even, we may add, in " the barren church of heathendom " (as it is called in one of the chants of the Orthodox Church)—we must remember that the Church is an object of faith, a revealed mystery, a manifold

beyond human experience, a spiritual organism,
" A body fitly joined together and compacted by
that which every joint supplieth, according to the
effectual working in the measure of every part "
(Eph. iv. 16).   It is of the Church as the ground
and basis of the world that it is said that God
chose " us in him (Christ) before the foundation
of the world " (Eph. i. 4) in " the fellowship of
the mystery, which from the beginning of the
world hath been hid in God, who created all
things by Jesus Christ : to the intent that now
unto the principalities and powers in heavenly
places might be known by the church the manifold wisdom of God, according to the eternal purpose which he purposed in Christ Jesus our Lord "
(Eph. iii. 9–11).   In this, as in other texts, the
Church is plainly delineated as divine Wisdom,
with its various aspects : as the heavenly Jerusalem, " coming down from God out of heaven,
prepared as a bride adorned for her husband "
(Rev. xxi. 2) ; as that " glory " which is given at
the prayer of Christ (Jn. xvii.) and " shall be
revealed in us " (Rom. viii. 18, 21) ; as the
" building of God " prepared for us, the " house
not made with hands, eternal in the heavens "
(2 Cor. v. 1) ; as " the kingdom prepared . . .
from the foundation of the world " (Mt. xxv. 34).
    The Church in the world is Sophia in process of

becoming, according to the double impulse of
creation and deification ; the former imposes the
conditions of the latter, the latter constitutes the
fulfilment of the former. God created the world
only that He might deify it and himself become
all in all to it.

The world has already, in principle, become
godly in becoming Churchly, through the twofold
revelation inseparably and unconfusedly effected
by the two revelatory persons of the Godhead
in the incarnation of the Word and the descent
of the Holy Ghost. Thus by reference to these
two mysteries its definition in terms of Wisdom
displays particularly clearly what is the nature of
the Church. And this identification—not without distinction—we find made in the Word of God.

There the Church is styled, in the first place,
" the body of Christ " : " Now ye are the body
of Christ, and members in particular " (1 Cor.
xii. 29), the Church " is his body, the fullness of
him that filleth all in all " (Eph. i. 23 ; cf. iv. 12,
and Col. i. 24). Such definitions are to be taken
not as a mere comparison, a kind of metaphor,
but in the most realistic sense. The Church is
the Body of Christ in virtue of his Incarnation :
it is the universal human nature of the second
Adam, created Wisdom, inseparably and unconfusedly united in him with his divine nature, that

divine Wisdom which is " the fullness of him that filleth all in all ". It is in virtue of this participation with Christ in his state of Incarnation that the apostle Paul could say, in the name of every believing soul : " I live ; yet, not I, but Christ liveth in me " (Gal. ii. 20). Another mystical expression of the essence of the Church given in the Word of God is that it is the Bride or Spouse of Christ (2 Cor. xi. 2 ; Rev. xix. 7–8 ; xxi. 9 ; xxii. 7). Actually this expression has its origin in the Old Testament, in the Song of Songs, that most mysterious and most " New Testament " book in the whole Bible, and in the prophets (Is. liv. 6 ; lxii. 4 ; Ezek. xvi.). The mystical marriage there described is shewn to be a mystery " concerning Christ and the Church " (Eph. v. 32).

The relation between bride and bridegroom, and more especially between husband and wife, is defined as a bond of love joining two in one life, " one flesh " (Gen. ii. 24 ; Mt. xix. 5–6 ; x. 8). Accordingly it is applied to the Incarnation ; directly to the mutual relation between Christ and his mother, the " unwedded Bride " ; more remotely in general to the soul of every man. In terms of Wisdom this figure implies that the Word, who is himself the Wisdom of God, exercises a loving domination over the created

Wisdom, uniting it to himself and thereby deifying it. But the latter is not thereby deprived of its own life, either natural or personal—in its multiple created personifications. And this love is mutual, though unequal ; since Christ is the head ; for as the husband is the head of the wife, so is Christ the head of the Church espoused to him (Eph. v).

But besides this, the Church is further defined in relation to the Holy Ghost ; to live in the Church is to be enlightened by his grace. The Church is therefore not only the body of Christ, but also the temple of the Holy Ghost : " Know ye not that ye are the temple of God, and that the Spirit of God dwelleth in you ? " (1 Cor. iii. 16–17 ; vi. 19 ; 2 Cor. vi. 16 ; Eph. xxi. 22. Compare also the whole account of the working of the Holy Ghost through the Apostles in the book of the Acts. And here we should recall that it is by the Holy Ghost that all the sacraments and sacramentals of the Church are accomplished, and especially the eucharistic change, μεταβολή, as indicated in the epiklesis.) We know already what is the basis of this conjoint revelation of the Son and the Spirit in the Church. It is one and the same revelation, effected by the twofold mission of the two divine persons from the Father to the world. This it is which makes the Church the revelation, in terms of created Wisdom, of the divine.

This union initiated by the incarnation and the descent of the Holy Ghost is primarily sacramental. That is to say, it is accomplished primarily by means of the sacraments and above all by means of the holy Eucharist. Though, of course, the sacraments form the regular channel of communion with God, they are by no means the only channel in such a sense as would exclude all others. We may say that in the present age the Church is the body of Christ precisely as being that eucharistic body on which are bestowed the eucharistic gifts of the Holy Ghost, the giver of life in Christ. To the Church as a whole the plenitude of the manifestations of divine Wisdom is present. Accordingly it is granted not only full communion with God in Christ in the power of the Holy Spirit, but also full communion in the divine and the created Wisdom of God. This latter is disclosed to the Church in the person of the Mother of God, together with the whole of the Church triumphant, angels and saintly men. The full significance of the sophianic character of the Church cannot be restricted to its relation to Christ, or defined, so to speak, Christo-centrically. That is why Protestantism is at fault in denying, as it commonly does, the proper place in the life of the Church which belongs to created Wisdom or, as we may say, without prejudice, to the *communio Sanctorum*, with the Mother of God at their head. In virtue of the common life of the Church we find the stream of Wisdom flowing at every source into the glorified creation. But the reception of this fullness of the life of the Church is impaired wherever there is, if not a complete denial of the holiness of the Mother of God and the saints, and of the veneration due to them, yet some measure of defect in that veneration.

On the grounds we have mentioned it is thus impossible to confine the Church to the limits of the world of men alone. We are bound to include in it that nature with which mankind is united. With the fall of man, " the creation was made subject to vanity " (Rom. viii. 20), and from his glorification it must await its own. The blessings provided for such natural and artificial objects as water, fruit and buildings, considered as the first stage in their penetration by Wisdom *in the power of the Holy Spirit*, yield clear evidence of the activity of the Church beyond the limits of the world of men. This is the preparation of nature for that transfiguration of all things, when there shall be revealed " new heavens and a new earth " wherein justice may dwell.

The Church is the heart and essence of the world, its hidden final cause. Above all it is the treasury of the gifts of grace, the source of eternal life and salvation. It is the guardian of the sacraments through that power of life which it derives by the " apostolic succession " from Christ. All this has, of course, always been taught in the doctrine of the Church. Yet there is a further cosmic, historical, and eschatological side to it to which we must give explicit expression here. The Church, since it is God-manhood in history, and develops through history, is inseparable from the life of mankind in time. Mankind itself may forsake the Church and relapse into bondage under the elements of the world (Gal. iv. 3) or to itself. Our own age with its pagan naturalism and humanist idolatry of man provides a clear example of this. But the exaggerations of error cannot abrogate that truth which they pervert. And the truth remains, that man was really made to be lord of creation. He is called to lead the whole creation up to the glory of God ; and if in his fall he became instead enslaved to it, yet in Christ this servitude is thrown off by the power of the Spirit. The Satanic principle in man is only strengthened by his unspiritual technical conquest of nature " in his own name ". But there is still the possibility of a good and true humani-

zation of nature, accomplished in the name of
Christ, and this forms part of those " works "
which are to be done in his name by those
that believe in him (Jn. xiv. 12). In and
through the Church, the conquest of the forces of
nature, which is at present an unspiritual magic,
can become Christian theurgy. Through man
created Wisdom can inform the formless elements,
the *tohu-bohu* of matter, till it becomes an extension of man's own body.

This is not to deny the original confidence of
Christianity that heaven and earth are, at the
end of this age, to be transfigured by the hand of
the Lord. But that in its turn does not affect the
necessity we are under of admitting that, *until*
that transfiguration, all in history can and must
be wrought out by man in human fashion. For
in God-manhood is included the whole fullness
of manhood, with its freedom and creativity. At
the present time there hangs over the whole
economic and industrial process the curse of
secularism—that product of the new age (for in
earlier periods of history, as well in heathen as
in Christian cultures, economic activity was
governed by values at bottom religious, and thus
to some extent, at any rate, sanctified).

The secularist divorce of the human from the
divine principle in man, with its sequel in the

idolatry of the human, is an error ; but equally false is the denial of the human principle in the name of the divine. For the divine-human character of the Church involves the complete union of both principles. A sophianic conception of the world renders impossible any such Manichean denial of the world as would treat it as evil and destined only to destruction, leaving man nothing to aspire to but to flee the world, in the endeavour to become an unworldly, a discarnate being. In the same way, a sophianic conception of the Church necessarily extends to its power over nature, symbolized in all those benedictions which the Church itself employs. Nature is not alien to the Church ; it belongs to it.

Still less can the general creativity of man be allowed to be thus alien to the Church. A stream of influence long dominant brought to bear on human creativity an ascetic conception of Christianity, almost Manichean—and certainly far from sophianic—a conception generally suspicious of and at times frankly opposed to all such creativity, seeing in it no more than a Satanic self-aggrandisement and the surrender of man to the prince of this world. Evidently, however, we can also discern another fact to be set against this ; the history of Christianity has marked a flowering of human creativity ; for Christianity gave man spiritual freedom, and thereby liberated the creative element in him. The periods of dogmatic and liturgical creation were marked by a luxuriant flowering of all the creative powers of man. But for some time now a fatal cleavage has been apparent in this field ; the development of creativity in humanism followed the course of a really Satanic temptation to self-idolatry. And in face of this Christianity necessarily appeared to occupy a defensive, apologetic position. So humanism remains up to the present pagan ; whereas in truth it should belong to Christianity ; and in this sense the true humanism has yet to appear. Yet it remains true that human creativity— thought, science, art—is in its data and its principles sophianic. It is the revelation of Wisdom through mankind, and its reception in the world. Only a sophianic world-view can establish and justify the creative mission of man, made known to him in the fact of his manhood with all its creative capacities. The discovery of a mode of creativity which shall be at the same time " Churchly " and free, with Christ and in Christ, inspired by the Spirit of God, is the task set to our generation. And that, too, is the legacy of the dogma of Chalcedon on the union of the divine with human nature, each in its full perfection, in Christ and consequently also in his Church.

Man's creativity is given him that he may humanize himself to the limit, before this age declines to its end. For the ripening of history, too, is a process of fulfilment, hurrying towards that coming springtide of the last days, when " the branch (of the fig-tree) is yet tender, and putteth forth leaves " (Mt. xxiv. 32).

In man creation is to become aware of its own sophianic character and recognize it in intelligence, the seminal reason of creation, and its flower. And therewith man will recognize the likeness of the wisdom of God in himself.

Repentance for sin and the redemption bestowed by Christ do not paralyse, but on the contrary liberate the creative powers of man. Thereby man, in virtue of the image of God within him, recognizes his own communal existence, not as an individual, but in the union of humanity in the bond of its own common nature and of a subsistent love. Such is the Church ; a divine-human community. Such is the *sobornost'* of its mystical life. Such, too, in consequence, the *sociality* of its historical life. We may say that all in the inner life of the Church is *soborny*, all its outward life is social. The heart of all the various forms which we find sociality assuming in communal life and in culture is the manifestation of this inward community, this *mutuality* whereby

mankind is unified to such a point that love for
God and for the neighbour are inseparable and
the second commandment is " like unto " the
first (Mt. xxii. 39).

A consequence of this fact is the social mission
of the Church, which leads it to extend its solici-
tude to, and to accept responsibility for, the redemption not only of the individual personality,
but also of social life. This is not merely the
practical application of Christian ethics or an
opportune adaptation to the demand of the day :
it is of the very essence of the Church. For in
reality mankind is more than a mere congeries
of atomic individuals, more than their mechanical
coagulation, not an aggregate but an organism ;
the body of the Church, the body of Christ.
Sociality as a fact of nature is to-day considered
to be obnoxious to Christianity or, at any rate,
irrelevant to it. But this is only a temporary misunderstanding : within, and even outside the
Church, there is a growing understanding of the
truth that " without me ye can do nothing "
(Jn. xv. 5), for sociality is the sophianic development of mankind through history. And though
the powers of evil will guard to the end the force
of their temptation towards separation ; yet " the
saints shall reign with Christ " even outwardly
in history (Apoc. xx. 1–6).

The elements of this world, the " beast " in continual rebellion against the influence of Wisdom, appear at their strongest in the State. This appears to be a kind of callosity on the skin of the social body—the Great Wen. And if it may be accepted by the Church (Rom. xiii.) and even receive from it a conditional consecration on the supposition that the beast is really tamed and docile ; yet the beast remains by nature untameable. Continually it aspires to become " totalitarian ", and to effect the complete and unlimited triumph of its bestiality.

Therefore the State bears the likeness of " the beast that ascendeth out of the bottomless pit ", and, as such, it blasphemes all that is holy. Between it and the Church there can be no peace, the beast of the State " the Lord shall consume with the spirit of his mouth " (2 Thess. ii. 5), it will be overthrown and annihilated in " the kingdom of the saints ", though this itself be but a temporary, and, as it were, symbolic, triumph of the Church on earth. But it is in conflict with the beast that the Church appears in its true colours as a community united on the basis of love, not by any kind of constraint, which for the State, on the other hand, is only natural. Accordingly any concordat between Church and State can only be a compromise, necessarily embarrassing to the Church, which must always remain in relation to the State an anarchic force.

The history of the humanity of Christ is the history of the Church as it is figured in the Apocalypse. The apocalyptic content of history is the drama of the world conflict between the forces of Christ and those of Antichrist. And since Christ is conqueror, therefore it is the history of his victory and his conquest, the triumph of the kingdom of God. This can also be presented in the sense of a struggle between two rival principles ; between the true Sophia which irradiates the world with wisdom, and the forces of evil, " Sophia fallen ". The " woman clothed with the sun " and pursued by the dragon is opposed to " the great whore ", " Babylon the great, the mother of harlots and abominations of the earth " (Rev. xvii. 5. With which compare the analogous figures of Proverbs vii. 6–27 ; and ix. 13–18).

This is not the place to enter into the necessary discussion of that nicest question of theology, the problem of the nature of evil. Evil is a parasite, possessing no substantive title to existence, but subsisting by means of the *confusion* of good and evil, as shadows, and darkness itself, are only apparent by contrast with the light. The overcoming and suppression of evil therefore consists in *separating* it from good, whereupon it must inevitably languish and die. This separation is to be effected only by the ending of history, which accordingly appears in this respect to be a process of dialectic including sophianic and anti-sophianic moments. In history the accession of Christ to the kingdom of God, which is the accomplishment of the Holy Spirit, is to take place upon the descent from heaven of the new Jerusalem. This is a figure of the union of the created with divine Wisdom. The whole world is coming to be the Church; wherefore in the new city there will be no temple (Rev. xxi. 22); for therein divine Wisdom, the diunity of the Son and the Spirit, is manifest in the created.

Only in the light of sophiology can we grasp all the scope of that eschatological fulfilment of all things, which is not limited to the final separation of good and evil in the last Judgment at the end of this age, but, in ways invisible to us, transcends even that separation, for then God shall be all in all, and divine Wisdom fulfilled in the created. This accomplishment has an inner inevitability and predeterminacy, which yet does not suppress created freedom. For that freedom is not substantive but rather modal; it determines not the " what " but the " how ", not the existence and final issue of the cosmic process, but only the manner of its accomplishment. All the positive wealth of being of any creature lies in its sophianic content. Certainly created freedom is allowed partially to immerse that content in " fallen " wisdom, but that can be only a transitory, not a definitive, condition. Wisdom, with its positive wealth of being, can compel by its attraction, " Not by might, nor by power, but by my spirit, saith the Lord of hosts " (Zech. iv. 6). Evil, like a shadow, possesses but an illusory existence, which sooner or later must disclose the vanity of its illusion. The liberty of the creature cannot stand out to the end against the compelling attraction of Wisdom, and its evident efficacity. This forms, so to speak, an " ontological argument " for the existence of Sophia, its constraining force. This power of persuasion is grounded in the long-suffering of God and wins its victories only by enduring much from the stubbornness of the creature.

The acceptance of this principle of sophianic determination by no means involves the denial of those torments " prepared for the devil and his angels " (Mt. xxv.) or of the freedom unto evil of those who still persist in self-assertion. But freedom unto evil has no substantive foundation, no resources to endure to eternity, and sooner or later must inevitably wither before the radiance of wisdom.

This is by no means the idea of *apokatastasis*, the re-establishment of all things. Such a notion is for the most part a misunderstanding, in so far as the term is applied in connection with the last things to the accomplishment of all that failed to find a place earlier in the history of the world. What we are speaking of here is in any case not *apokatastasis*, but pan-entheosis, or simply pan-theosis, the complete penetration of the creature by wisdom, the manifestation of the power of God-manhood in the whole world. For this to take place a necessary sophianic postulate is required, which is in fact realized, beyond the limits of this age, in those " ages of ages " the reality whereof, though beyond our comprehension, the Church unceasingly proclaims. There will be nothing violent or mechanical about this accomplishment, nothing to violate or set aside the liberty of the creature. But the latter cannot be set side by side with or over against divine Wisdom on a basis, so to speak, of *equal* competition ; for ontologically they are not equal. Yet, in effect, they are treated as equal by those who attribute the like degree and kind of perpetuity impartially to the work of wisdom in paradise and that of the forces opposed to it in hell.

The freedom of the rebellious creature cannot stand out to the end against the divine Wisdom on the empty resources of its own nothingness. For in reality there is but one true existence, the divine. There is only the one God in his divine Wisdom, and outside him nothing whatever. What is not God is *nothing*. Yet he does not constrain freedom ; he convinces it. It will be preserved inviolate even after the victory over the powers of hell. Yet that victory is to be won not by annihilation, as the theory of conditional immortality supposes, but by the liberation of those sophianic forces of life which are preserved even in the cramped and distorted existence of hell. And into the fullness of this unfolding of the riches of Wisdom there must of necessity enter all that finds its proper fulfilment through history, all the self-enlargement and self-conquest accomplished by mankind. For mankind can gain wisdom only in freedom, though it be created freedom, learning with its human will and energy, as the 6th General Council defined, to " imitate " the will of God.

Freedom is only a mode in which life is participated, not the content of life itself. That can consist only in one thing ; for the creature to receive and effect after its own manner, in freedom, and endlessly to prolong that realization of the divine in the created Sophia, which is the Church. " In wisdom hast thou made them all " (Ps. 104). [1]

[1] Only the very broadest outlines of apocalyptic and eschatology are indicated here. It remains for the author to fill them in in the third part of his study of the foundations of sophiology, now preparing for the press.

BIBLIOGRAPHY OF THE SOPHIOLOGICAL WORKS OF SERGIUS BULGAKOV

EARLY PREPARATORY WORKS : 1–3

1. *From Marxism to Idealism.* Collected Articles (1896–1903). S. Petersburg 1903. Pp. 21+347. *Russian.*
2. *Two Cities.* Inquiries on the nature of social idealism. Vol. I–II. Moscow 1911. Pp. 21+303+313. *Russian.*
3. *The Philosophy of Economics*, Part I : The World as Economics. Moscow 1912. Pp. 4+321. *Russian.*

4. *The Light that Never Fades.* Intuitions and speculations. Moscow 1917. Pp. 4+417. *Russian.*
5. *Calm Meditations.* Collected articles (1911–1915). Moscow 1918. Pp. 202. *Russian.*
6. *Person and Personality.* Scholia to *The Light that Never Fades.* Praha 1925 (in Symposium in honour of P. B. Struve). *Russian.*

THE FIRST SOPHIOLOGICAL TRILOGY : 7–9

7. *The Burning Bush.* Paris 1927. Pp. 290. YMCA press. *Russian.*
8. *The Friend of the Bridegroom.* Paris 1928. Pp. 276. Published by the Author. *Russian.*
9. *Jacob's Ladder.* Paris 1929. Pp. 229. Published by the Author. *Russian.*
10. *Chapters on the Trinity.* " Orthodox Thought " No. 1. and No. 2. Paris 1928 and 1930. P. 58+29. Editions of the Theological Institute.=Capita de Trinitate. Internationale Kirchliche Zeitschrift, 1936. *Russian.*

11. *The Eucharistic Dogma.* " Puit " No's. 20 and 21. Paris 1930. Pp. 44+30. *Russian.*
12. *Icons and their Veneration.* Paris 1931. Pp. 166. YMCA press. *Russian.*
13. *The Legacy of St. Sergius to Russian Theology.* " Puit " No. 5. Paris 1926. Pp. 18. *Russian.*
14. *On Miracles in the Gospel.* Paris 1932. Pp. 115. YMCA press. *Russian.*
15. *L'Orthodoxie.* Paris 1932. Pp. 276. F. Alcan. (English and Rumanian translations.)
16. *Die Tragœdie der Philosophie.* Darmstadt. 1927. Pp. 327.
17. *Die Kosmodizee.* " Das Oestliche Christentum." 1925.
18. *The Name of God.* A Theological inquiry into the philosophy of the word. (Only the first chapter of this work is published in German : *Was ist das Wort* in Festschrift, Th. G. Masarix. 1930.)

THE SECOND AND CHIEF SOPHIOLOGICAL TRILOGY : 1–3

1. *The Lamb of God. On God-manhood.* Part I. YMCA press, Paris 1933. Pp. 11+468+5. *Russian.*
2. *The Comforter. On God-manhood.* Part. II. YMCA press, Paris 1936. Pp. 447+2. *Russian.*
3. The third (eschatological) part is in preparation.
4. *The Lamb of God.* A review by the author. " Puit," No. 41, Paris 1934. Pp. 5. *Russian.*
5. Same in English. " Theology," No. 163. Jan. 1934, London. Pp. 4.
6. *The Comforter.* A review by the author. " Puit," No. 50, Paris 1936. Pp. 4. *Russian.*
7. *The Spirit of Dogma.* (After Seven Occumenical Councils.) Speech at the Convocation of the Russian Orthodox Theological Seminary, 1932. " Puit," No. 37, Paris 1933. Pp. 35. *Russian.*
8. *The Holy Grail.* (An essay on a dogmatic exegesis of John xix, 34.) " Puit," No. 32, 1932, Paris. Pp. 42. *Russian.*

9. *On Sophia, the Wisdom of God.* Ukaze of the Moscow Patriarchate, and reports of the Rev. Prof. Sergius Bulgakov to the Metropolitan Eulogius. YMCA press, Paris 1935. Pp. 64. *Russian.* Same in German: Autorität und Freiheit in der rusischers Kirche. "Orient Und Occident," Heft 1, Neue Folge, März 1936. Pp. 27.

10. *More on the Problem of Sophia the Wisdom of God.* (With reference to the decision of the Bishops' Council in Karlovtsi.) YMCA press, Paris 1936. Pp. 24. Also in "Puit," No. 50, 1936. *Russian.*

11. *Zur Frage nach der Weisheit Gottes.* Thesem zum Vortrag über die Sophiologie, vorgelegt auf der english-russischen Theologienkonferenz in Mirfield, am 28 April 1936, Kyrios 1936. Keftz.

12. *Die Christliche Anthropologie.* "Kirche, Staat und Mensch," (Russisch-Orthodoxen Sammelwerk zur Vorbereitung der Weltkirchenkonferenz von 1937.)

13. *Social Teaching in Modern Russian Orthodox Theology.* The Twentieth Annual Hale Memorial Sermon. Seabury Western Theological Seminary, Evanston Ill. U.S.A., 1934. Pp.20.

14. *The Problem of Conditional Immortality.* ("Puit" The Way, 1937, N.N. 1-2.) *Russian.*

15. *From Marxism to Sophiology.* (The Review of Religion.) Vol. I, No. 4, May 1937. Columbia University Press, New York. (Annual Address delivered at Columbia University, October 27, 1936.)